HEBREWS

JESUS IS BETTER

HEBREWS

JESUS IS BETTER

STORYTELLER

Lifeway Press®
Nashville, Tennessee

Editorial Team

Cynthia Hopkins
Writer

Angel Prohaska
Associate Editor

Reid Patton
Senior Editor

Jon Rodda
Art Director

Tyler Quillet
Managing Editor

Joel Polk
Publisher, Small Group Publishing

Brian Daniel
Director, Adult Ministry Publishing

ISBN: 978-1-0877-6336-1 • Item number: 005837545
Dewey decimal classification: 227.87 • Subject heading: BIBLE. N.T. HEBREWS / JESUS CHRIST / CHARACTERS AND CHARACTERISTICS IN THE BIBLE

To order additional copies of this resource, write to Lifeway Resources Customer Service; 200 Powell Place, Suite 100, Brentwood, TN 37027; fax 615-251-5933; call toll free 800-458-2772; order online at Lifeway.com; or email orderentry@lifeway.com.

Printed in the United States of America

Adult Ministry Publishing • Lifeway Resources • 200 Powell Place • Brentwood, TN 37027

CONTENTS

ABOUT STORYTELLER

God could've chosen to reveal Himself in any way that He desired, yet in His wisdom, He chose to reveal Himself in the context of a story. We come to know and understand this reality as we immerse ourselves in the Scriptures and begin to see the entirety of Scripture as one interconnected story. By becoming familiar with the individual stories of Scripture, we train ourselves to see each as one part of God's big story.

Storyteller is a six week devotional and group Bible study experience designed to take people through Scripture in a way that is beautiful, intuitive, and interactive. Each volume uses a book of the Bible or a portion of Scripture from within a book to examine a key theme. This theme guides the Bible study experience and gives readers handles to help understand and digest what they're reading.

At the end of each study, you should have a deeper understanding of God, His Word, the big themes of Scripture, the connectedness of God's story, and His work in your life.

Let's enter the story together.

ABOUT HEBREWS

AUTHOR

Unique among New Testament books, the author of Hebrews is unknown. Even though the author's identity is lost to time, we know that early Christians received this letter as an inspired part of Scripture in the first century. We do know that the author was a second-generation Christian (2:3), that he knew Timothy (13:23), and that the recipients of the letter were known to him (3:12; 7:5; 13:22). Additionally, because of the author's familiarity with the Old Testament as well as the Jewish sacrificial system, we can conclude the author came from a Jewish background. Biblical scholars have proposed authors including Luke, Clement of Rome, Barnabas, Apollos, Peter, Silas, and Jude.

BACKGROUND

Hebrews was likely written to a group of Jewish Christians who were considering a return to Judaism because of the increasing persecution they were experiencing. This is perhaps why the author included the so-called "warning passages" about the spiritual danger of turning your back on Jesus (Hebrews frequently encourages the audience to endure and warns against leaving Christ, see 2:1-4; 3:7–4:13; 5:11–6:12; 10:19-39; 12:1-29). The "letter" to the Hebrews includes no traditional greeting or stated purpose one finds in other New Testament letters. As such, it is best understood as a sermon meant to be shared and circulated within the church.

DATE

The book was likely written prior to the destruction of Jerusalem in AD 70 because if that had happened, it would have been mentioned. Clement of Rome quoted the book in AD 96, so we know that it was written before then. The author mentions public persecution in 10:32-34. Roman emperors Nero and Domitian both persecuted the church during their reigns. The most likely date for the later is during the persecution of Nero (AD 54–68).

PURPOSE

The letter to the Hebrews is a tribute to Jesus and an encouragement to persecuted Christians. The author had two goals: 1. Demonstrate that Jesus is incomparable—He is better than anything or anyone we could place our faith in. 2. Urge wavering followers of Jesus to pursue growth and maturity in Jesus Christ.

SIMPLIFIED OUTLINE[1]

The Superiority of Jesus (1:1–2:18)
The Superiority of Jesus's Faithfulness (3:1–4:16)
The Superiority of Jesus's Work (5:1–6:20)
The Superiority of Jesus's Priesthood (7:1–10:39)
The Superiority of Faith in Jesus (11:1–12:2)
The Superiority of God's Plan (12:3-29)
The Superiority of Life Following Jesus (13:1-25)

TIMELINE OF SELECT NEW TESTAMENT EVENTS

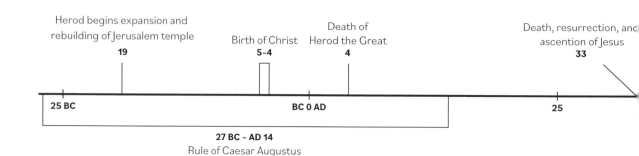

Herod begins expansion and
rebuilding of Jerusalem temple
19

Birth of Christ
5–4

Death of
Herod the Great
4

Death, resurrection, and
ascension of Jesus
33

25 BC

BC 0 AD

25

27 BC – AD 14
Rule of Caesar Augustus

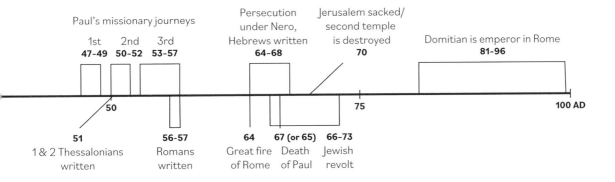

Paul's missionary journeys

1st
47-49

2nd
50-52

3rd
53-57

Persecution
under Nero,
Hebrews written
64-68

Jerusalem sacked/
second temple
is destroyed
70

Domitian is emperor in Rome
81-96

50

75

100 AD

51
1 & 2 Thessalonians
written

56-57
Romans
written

64
Great fire
of Rome

67 (or 65)
Death
of Paul

66-73
Jewish
revolt

WHY STUDY HEBREWS?

The letter to the Hebrews was written to a group of Jewish converts to Christianity who were considering abandoning Jesus and returning to Judaism. They were enduring persecution. Life was difficult, and they wondered if following Jesus was really worth it.

You may not be in their situation, but you know the feeling. You've likely been tempted to ask the same question—is Jesus worth it?

The author of Hebrews answers that question with an invitation—consider Jesus.

Take the time to know Him and see what He offers. Throughout Hebrews, the author systematically works through key themes and characters in the Bible and points out how Jesus is better than all of those things.

Let's walk together as we look at the One Hebrews describes as "the radiance of God's glory and the exact expression of [God's] nature, [Who sustains] all things by his powerful word" (1:3). You will not be disappointed.

1. Malcolm B. Yarnell III, "Hebrews," in *CSB Study Bible: Notes*, ed. Edwin A. Blum and Trevin Wax (Nashville, TN: Holman Bible Publishers, 2017), 1945–1946.

HOW TO USE THIS STUDY

Each week follows a repeated rhythm to guide you in your study of Hebrews and was crafted with lots of white space and photographic imagery to facilitate a time of reflection on Scripture.

The week begins with an introduction to the themes of the week. Throughout each week you'll find Scripture readings, devotions, and beautiful imagery to guide your time.

WEEK 3

BETTER HOPE

Each week includes five days of Scripture reading along with a short devotional thought and three questions to process what you've read.

The Scripture reading is printed out for you with plenty of space for you to take notes, circle, underline, and interact with the passage.

The sixth day contains no reading beyond a couple of verses to give you time to pause and listen to what God has said through the Scriptures this week. You may be tempted to skip this day all together, but resist this temptation. Sit and be quiet with God—even if it's only for a few minutes.

The seventh day each week offers a list of open-ended questions that apply to any passage of Scripture. Use this day to reflect on your own or meet with a group to discuss what you've learned. Take intentional time to remember and reflect on what the story of Hebrews is teaching you.

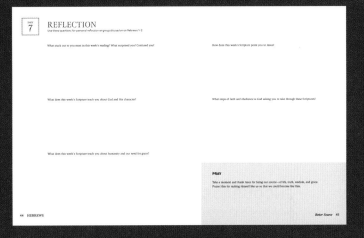

Throughout each week of study, you will notice callout boxes or supplemental pages provided to give greater context and clarity to the Scripture you're reading. These features will help you connect Hebrews to the bigger story of Scripture.

LEADING A GROUP

Each week of study contains a set of questions that can be used for small group meetings. These open-ended questions are meant to guide discussion of the week's Scripture passage. No matter the size of your group, here are some helpful tips for guiding discussion.

PREPARE

REVIEW the Scripture and your answers to the week's questions ahead of time.

PRAY over your group as well as the Scriptures you've been studying. Ask God's Spirit for help to lead the group deeper into God's truth and deeper in relationship with one another.

MINIMIZE DISTRACTIONS

We live in a time when our attention is increasingly divided. Try to see your group time as a space and respite from the digital clutter—from scrolling, notifications, likes, and newsfeeds. Commit to one another to give focused time and attention to the discussion at hand and minimize outside distractions. Help people focus on what's most important: connecting with God, with the Bible, and with one another.

ENCOURAGE DISCUSSION

A good small group experience has the following characteristics.

EVERYONE IS INCLUDED. Your goal is to foster a community where people are welcome just as they are but encouraged to grow spiritually.

EVERYONE PARTICIPATES. Encourage everyone to ask questions, share, or read aloud.

NO ONE DOMINATES. Even though you may be "leading" the group, try to see yourself as a participant steering the conversation rather than a teacher imparting information.

DON'T RUSH. Don't feel that a moment of silence is a bad thing. People may need time, and we should be glad to give it to them. Don't feel like you have to ask all the questions or stay away from questions that aren't included. Be sensitive to the Holy Spirit and to one another. Take your time.

INPUT IS AFFIRMED AND FOLLOWED UP. Make sure you point out something true or helpful in a response. Don't just move on. Build community with follow-up questions, asking other people to share when they have experienced similar things or how a truth has shaped their understanding of God and the Scripture you're studying. Conversation stalls when people feel that you don't want to hear their answers or that you're looking for only a certain answer. Engagement and affirmation keeps the conversation going.

GOD AND HIS WORD ARE CENTRAL. The questions in this study are meant to steer the conversation back to God, His Word, and the work of the gospel in our lives. Opinions and experiences are valuable and can be helpful, but God is the center of the Bible, the center of our story, and should be the center of our discussion. Trust Him to lead the discussion. Continually point people to the Word and to active steps of faith.

KEEP CONNECTING

Spiritual growth occurs in the context of community. Think of ways to connect with group members during the week. Your group will be more enjoyable the more you get to know one another through time spent outside of an official group meeting. The more people are comfortable with and involved in one another's lives, the more they'll look forward to being together. When people move beyond being friendly to truly being friends who form a community, they come to each session eager to engage instead of merely attending. Reserve time each week to touch base with individual group members.

WEEK 1

BETTER SOURCE

Go to the Source.

Hebrews is a sermon that was given to people who didn't fit in. Being a Christian meant living in a way that was very different from the norm, most notably in practices of faith and morality. In the first-century Roman world, when Hebrews was written, people worshiped anything and everything, including their Roman emperors. Christians stood out against that backdrop. On their best days, they were hated; on their worst days, they were publicly abused and executed.

Life was hard.

It was so hard, in fact, that some Christians started considering going back to Judaism. Judaism was an officially recognized religion to Romans, therefore a growing number of Christians believed that returning to their old ways would make things easier. It was a compromise they thought made sense.

So a Christian leader who loved them gave them the message we now read in Hebrews. He wanted them to know that there is only one Source of life and fulfillment, and there can be no compromise. No matter what solutions they might try to adopt—past, present, or future—Jesus is better.

He's better than all the answers our culture comes up with today, too. We try to be good enough. We make sacrifices of great cost. We trust in family, friends, jobs, ideas, and even politicians. None of those allegiances can sustain us. They always come up short.

There's only one starting point for any hope of knowing God and experiencing life in Him. His name is Jesus.

HEBREWS 1:1-4

THE NATURE OF THE SON

1 Long ago God spoke to our ancestors by the prophets at different times and in different ways. [2] In these last days, he has spoken to us by his Son. God has appointed him heir of all things and made the universe through him. [3] The Son is the radiance of God's glory and the exact expression of his nature, sustaining all things by his powerful word. After making purification for sins, he sat down at the right hand of the Majesty on high. [4] So he became superior to the angels, just as the name he inherited is more excellent than theirs.

THE GREATEST REVELATION

Think about the most magnificent part of creation you've ever seen. People travel great distances to see firsthand the enormity of the Grand Canyon and the power of Niagara Falls. We'll learn how to snorkel so we can explore the beauty of the Great Barrier Reef. We'll drive up narrow passes and endure altitude sickness to experience the most scenic mountain views. We do this because we want to experience something greater. We want to see glimpses of God.

The book of Hebrews begins with a reality that is beyond the wonder of the most wonderful sights on earth. It is the greatest reality of all.

God wants to reveal Himself to us even more than we want to see Him. And He has revealed Himself to us, through far more than His creation. A long time ago, He raised up prophets to reveal Himself to people. These men and women were passionate and powerful speakers, but at the end of the day, they were just men and women. Now, He has spoken to us in the most superior way of all—through Jesus His Son.

To see and hear Jesus was to see and hear God in the flesh. Jesus was active in the creation of all things, like the Grand Canyon, ocean reefs, and all those other places we'll go out of our way to see. And as co-Creator with God, He is a better revelation of God than any created thing. Jesus is superior to the prophets, too. He is the appointed Heir of all beings. It is through Jesus that God pursues us and all other sinful, lost people.

Jesus is the absolute fullest revelation of who God is and what He is like. God will never speak to us more clearly than He does through Jesus. We are right to respond with awe to God's creation, but there is nothing more awe-inspiring than God Himself, revealed to us in Jesus Christ. If we want to see God, then we must look to Jesus. He is the greatest reality of all. Nothing and no one can bring us closer to God than He can.

God will never speak to you more clearly
than He does through Jesus.

REFLECTIONS

How is Jesus described in verse 3? What does that teach us about His identity?

Name a few relationships, pursuits, objects, or hopes that you have sometimes treated as the greatest reality of your life. Why is Jesus better than those things?

God speaks to us most clearly through Jesus. What is your responsibility in hearing and receiving that message?

TRACING THE STORY

The original audience of Hebrews were men and women who had heard the gospel through the earliest followers of Jesus (2:3). Public persecution was a very real part of their lives (10:32-34). It is likely that this persecution was taking place under the Roman emperor Nero (AD 64–68), just before the destruction of the temple in Jerusalem. Hardship and suffering provide a backdrop for this letter.

HEBREWS 1:5-14

THE SON SUPERIOR TO ANGELS

[5] For to which of the angels did he ever say,

> You are my Son;
>
> today I have become your Father,

or again,

> I will be his Father,
>
> and he will be my Son?

[6] Again, when he brings his firstborn into the world, he says,

> And let all God's angels worship him.

[7] And about the angels he says:

> He makes his angels winds,
>
> and his servants a fiery flame,

[8] but to the Son:

> Your throne, God,
>
> is forever and ever,
>
> and the scepter of your kingdom
>
> is a scepter of justice.
>
> [9] You have loved righteousness
>
> and hated lawlessness;
>
> this is why God, your God,
>
> has anointed you
>
> with the oil of joy
>
> beyond your companions.

[10] And:

> In the beginning, Lord,
>
> you established the earth,
>
> and the heavens are the works
>
> of your hands;
>
> [11] they will perish, but you remain.
>
> They will all wear out like clothing;
>
> [12] you will roll them up like a cloak,
>
> and they will be changed like clothing.
>
> But you are the same,
>
> and your years will never end.

[13] Now to which of the angels has he ever said:

> Sit at my right hand
>
> until I make your enemies your footstool?

[14] Are they not all ministering spirits sent out to serve those who are going to inherit salvation?

UNIQUELY SUPERIOR

The sermon we now know as the book of Hebrews would have caught people's attention right from the start. To hear that someone was superior to the angels would have left Jewish Christians experiencing some measure of internal conflict.

This tension might seem odd to modern readers, but most first-century Jews exalted angels because of their involvement in giving the Law to Moses at Mt. Sinai (Deuteronomy 33:2). They considered the Law to be God's supreme revelation. So the call to adjust their long held beliefs was jarring.

But the author of Hebrews argued Jesus is better than angels (and everything else). He makes his argument starting in verse 5 with a series of Old Testament quotations about Jesus from God. Each fact emphasizes Jesus's superiority to angels.

God never designated any angel as His Son. That title belongs to Jesus alone. Instead, the angels exist to serve and worship Jesus. He is the eternal Son and righteous Heir of the great King David, sitting forever at God's right hand—the place of supreme honor.

It boils down to this—angels are messengers but Jesus is the message. Angels communicated God's message, but Jesus communicates God's being. Jesus is worthy of our worship, angels are not.

We might not worship angels or exalt them above Jesus, but there are other religious things we prioritize in this way. Maybe we think that a certain style of music is required for us to truly worship. Maybe we uphold some religious experience in this same way. Or maybe we hang our spiritual growth on the backs of gifted Christian leaders, longing for some message that will give us the knowledge we seek. But true knowledge of God only comes to us through Jesus.

He is superior to any spiritual thing or any spiritual person we value. Everything and everyone else must take a back seat. Jesus reveals God finally and without equivocation. He is the only way we can understand God's character and the central message of the Scriptures—the gospel.

Jesus is superior to any spiritual thing you value.

REFLECTIONS

Reread the verses on the previous page. According to these verses, why is Jesus superior to angels? List the ways you find below.

How can you tell if you're elevating a secondary or tertiary belief or preference to be more important than Jesus?

What is something (or someone) associated with your spiritual beliefs or faith practices that you might wrongly prioritize as more important than Jesus Himself?

INSIGHTS

In the Bible, the terms *angel* or *angels* occur nearly 300 times, with approximately one-third of those occurrences in the Old Testament. They serve in numerous ways—ministering to followers of God (Hebrews 1:14), obeying God to carry out His purposes (Psalm 103:20-21), calling attention to God's greatness (Daniel 7:10), and acknowledging the worth of every follower of Jesus (Matthew 18:10). Angels are a vital God-appointed reality, yet Jesus is better.

HEBREWS 2:5-13

JESUS AND HUMANITY

[5] For he has not subjected to angels the world to come that we are talking about.

[6] But someone somewhere has testified:

> **What is man that you remember him,**
>
> **or the son of man that you care for him?**
>
> [7] **You made him lower than the angels**
>
> **for a short time;**
>
> **you crowned him with glory and honor**
>
> [8] **and subjected everything under his feet.**

For in **subjecting everything** to him, he left nothing that is not subject to him. As it is, we do not yet see **everything subjected** to him. [9] But we do see Jesus — **made lower than the angels for a short time** so that by God's grace he might taste death for everyone — **crowned with glory and honor** because he suffered death.

[10] For in bringing many sons and daughters to glory, it was entirely appropriate that God — for whom and through whom all things exist — should make the pioneer of their salvation perfect through sufferings. [11] For the one who sanctifies and those who are sanctified all have one Father. That is why Jesus is not ashamed to call them brothers and sisters, [12] saying:

> **I will proclaim your name to my brothers and sisters;**
>
> **I will sing hymns to you in the congregation.**

[13] Again, **I will trust in him.** And again, **Here I am with the children God gave me.**

GLORY AND HONOR RESTORED

Questions about God are natural and common, even among people who follow Him. We wonder things like, "If God loves us, then why do bad things happen?" and "If God is so good, why would He send anyone to hell?" There are myriad answers we might receive to those questions. But Hebrews 2 shows us that Jesus is always the better answer to every question about God that plagues us.

When God made the world, He gave human beings a culture mandate (Genesis 1:28). He wanted us to take responsibility for the world He created—to subdue it and fill it with more people who also bear His image. Humans were created to perpetuate His glory, but we chose to perpetuate sin instead.

But God wasn't finished; His glory will always win out in the end. Jesus became a man to do what we previously could not; He came to show what God is like. And, unlike every other person, Jesus never fails. He succeeded in the mission God gave Him.

Jesus shows us God's undistracted plan to redeem us. Because of sin's effects, that's hard for many people to understand. Even though the world was created by Jesus and for Jesus, we do not yet see the world in submission to Him. For that we have to wait for the ultimate fulfillment of our redemption. But the world will not always be as it is.

By God's design, all of history is headed toward its fulfillment in Jesus. His rule and reign was inaugurated at the cross, where Jesus stood in our place to bear the full weight of the penalty for our sins. God sent Jesus as a pioneer—a forerunner—to win the battle we could not win ourselves. And He accomplished this salvation through His suffering.

All of our suffering and hardship will be redeemed in the coming kingdom. Jesus is not ashamed to unite with us as brothers and sisters, because through His death He destroyed the power and source of our shame. He has made those who trust in Him perfectly clean and holy before God, and we will reign with Him forever.

If you want to know who God is, there is no better answer than Jesus.

If you want to know who God is,
there is no better answer than Jesus.

REFLECTIONS

What does it mean to be a pioneer? What does the author of Hebrews mean when he refers to Jesus as the "pioneer" of our salvation (v. 10)?

Think of a question about God's character that you have had at some point, or that someone has wondered aloud to you. How might looking to Jesus help you answer that question?

If you have placed your faith in Jesus, then He has made you His brother or sister. You are family. What is something you need Him to teach you? What is your responsibility in learning that lesson?

HEBREWS 2:14-16

[14] Now since the children have flesh and blood in common, Jesus also shared in these, so that through his death he might destroy the one holding the power of death — that is, the devil — [15] and free those who were held in slavery all their lives by the fear of death. [16] For it is clear that he does not reach out to help angels, but to help Abraham's offspring.

OVERTURNING FATE

In times of war or global pandemic, we become increasingly aware of our own mortality, no matter how young or old we might be. It might seem strange, but an awareness of death is actually a good thing. In easier days, we can slide through life without a thought about our mortality. But death is among the most central facts of every life.

It wasn't always.

God didn't create the first people to experience death. But when they chose to mistrust and reject God's loving instruction, death entered the picture as a byproduct of sin and corrupted all of our lives. All of the hardship in this life is inextricably linked to sin. And in a sinful world, death is actually a gift. Otherwise, we'd live forever in an imperfect, disintegrating place with unending struggle.

But death isn't the final word. Jesus came to make life, and death, better.

He became a man to help us overcome the reality of death that sin established. There was no other way to change the outcome for flesh-and-blood people than to become a flesh-and-blood person and make the sacrifice none of us were able to make. By God's grace-driven plan, Jesus's life, death, and resurrection flipped the script our sinful hearts had written.

Hebrews 2:15 contains a beautiful truth about what Jesus came to do for us. He came to "free those who were held in slavery all their lives by the fear of death." Jesus's death and resurrection have established a new reality for every person who trusts in Him—mortality no longer has the power to enslave us, because with death comes new and eternal life.

Jesus's life, death, and resurrection flipped
the script your sinful heart had written.

REFLECTIONS

These verses continue the author of Hebrews' discussion about angels. How are human beings different than angels? In the context of these verses, why does that matter?

What does it look like to live in fear of death?

What would it look like for you to live each day as someone who has been freed from the fear of death?

The Exaltation of
JESUS

The themes of Hebrews are echoed throughout Scripture. Seeing these connecting points help us connect to the big story of Scripture. Consider reading the following parallel passages that align with this week's reading.

HEBREWS 1:1-2

God made the universe through Jesus

GENESIS 1:26

COLOSSIANS 1:15-17

JOHN 1:1

HEBREWS 1:13-14

Angels communicated God's message, but Jesus communicates God's being

COLOSSIANS 1:16

JUDE 1:6

REVELATION 19:10

ISAIAH 6:3

HEBREWS 2:9

Jesus became a man to show us God's glory and honor

JOHN 1:14

PHILIPPIANS 2:7-11

HEBREWS 2:14-15

Jesus became a man to free us from the power of death

2 TIMOTHY 1:10

ROMANS 8:3

REVELATION 1:18

HEBREWS 2:18

Jesus suffered when He was tempted, so He is able to help those who are tempted

JUDE 1:24

1 CORINTHIANS 10:13

HEBREWS 2:17-18

[17] Therefore, he had to be like his brothers and sisters in every way, so that he could become a merciful and faithful high priest in matters pertaining to God, to make atonement for the sins of the people. [18] For since he himself has suffered when he was tempted, he is able to help those who are tempted.

DAY 5 SHARING EXPERIENCE

Affinity is one of the strongest foundations for friendship. We form deep relationships with those familiar with our experiences and interests because those things shape who we are. Sometimes when we walk through suffering and difficulty, though, we start to think our struggle is unique and no one can truly relate.

We extend this line of thinking to Jesus, minimizing His humanity for all sorts of reasons. We think, "Even though He came to earth as man, He is also God." Or we might think, "Jesus didn't have my parents." "He didn't have to deal with the temptations that come with the internet." "He wasn't married." And on and on the diminishing of His humanity goes.

But the truth is that Jesus is not distant from our experience, whatever that particular experience is. Being made like us doesn't mean that Jesus lived through every situation we encounter, but it does mean He has experienced what it is like to live in a broken world where things are not as they should be.

And it wasn't easy.

Jesus didn't just face a few temptations and easily overcome them, as if to say, "See? I'm perfect and you're not." No, Jesus suffered when He was tempted. So He empathizes with you when you face temptation, whatever that temptation happens to be. Not only that, but because He came as a man who suffered, He knows what it's like to suffer. He knows the strength needed to overcome temptation. He has been where you are, experiencing the pain and frustration of living in a world tainted by sin.

When you walk through dark days, know that you can turn to Jesus because He understands. He loves you enough to share in your experience. Whatever you're feeling, He lived it, and because of this He is able to speak to it with intimate knowledge and the greatest measure of relational affinity.

Jesus is not distant from your experience
whatever that experience is.

REFLECTIONS

Based on what you know or have read about Jesus, what are some ways He shared in human experiences (both good and bad)?

What does it tell you about Jesus that He "had to be like (you) in every way"? How should that truth impact your relationship with Him?

Jesus did not stop helping you when He finished His work on the cross or when He ascended to heaven. How has Jesus helped you recently?

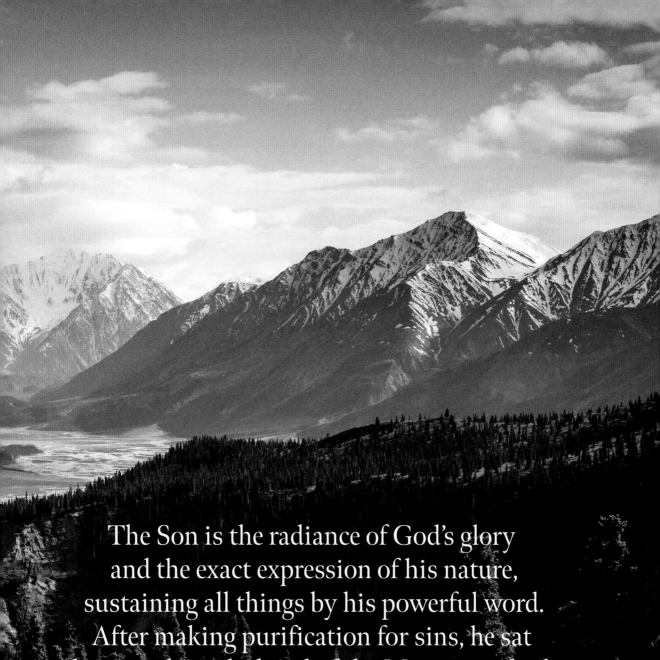

The Son is the radiance of God's glory
and the exact expression of his nature,
sustaining all things by his powerful word.
After making purification for sins, he sat
down at the right hand of the Majesty on high.

HEBREWS 1:3

REFLECTION

Use these questions for personal reflection or group discussion on Hebrews 1–2.

What stuck out to you most in this week's reading? What surprised you? Confused you?

What does this week's Scripture teach you about God and His character?

What does this week's Scripture teach you about humanity and our need for grace?

How does this week's Scripture point you to Jesus?

What steps of faith and obedience is God asking you to take through these Scriptures?

PRAY

Take a moment and thank Jesus for being our Source—of life, truth, wisdom, and grace. Praise Him for making Himself like us so that we could become like Him.

WEEK 2

BETTER LEADER

Follow the Leader.

We live in a culture that is fascinated with identifying "the best." New parents jump through hoops to get on long waiting lists at the "best" preschools. If we're traveling, we might search reviews to find the best burger, best pizza, or some other best food a city is known for. And radio and TV personalities engage in intense debates over who should be considered the best athlete, actor, musician, president, or world leader of all time.

The writer of Hebrews recognized this same tendency in the people of his day. It was hard to follow Jesus. Following Jesus's leadership required personal sacrifice. So they considered other leaders and wondered if following Jesus was the best option.

After all, Moses was a good leader, too. Moses had given them the Law. If they struggled to follow the rules Moses had helped to establish, there was a high priest to pick up the slack. Moses and the high priest had been considered their "best" leaders for centuries.

But Hebrews was written to assure them that living their spiritual lives vicariously through the leadership of Moses, the high priest, or any other person—no matter how faithful—was inferior and insufficient.

There is no better leader than Jesus. Not Moses or a high priest. Not Gandhi or Buddha or Confucius or Joseph Smith. Not the best business leader. Not your family. Not your pastor or favorite author.

That's not to say these people can't teach or lead us. They can. But, ultimately, their leadership is only effective to the extent that they point us to Jesus.

HEBREWS 3:1-6

OUR APOSTLE AND HIGH PRIEST

3 Therefore, holy brothers and sisters, who share in a heavenly calling, consider Jesus, the apostle and high priest of our confession. [2] He was faithful to the one who appointed him, just as Moses was in all God's household. [3] For Jesus is considered worthy of more glory than Moses, just as the builder has more honor than the house. [4] Now every house is built by someone, but the one who built everything is God. [5] Moses was faithful as a servant in all God's household, as a testimony to what would be said in the future. [6] But Christ was faithful as a Son over his household. And we are that household if we hold on to our confidence and the hope in which we boast.

CONSIDER JESUS

If it weren't for the phrase, "holy brothers and sisters," you might think these words were written to people who don't know Jesus. "Holy brothers and sisters" have already considered Jesus—considering Jesus is what led them to follow Him in the first place.

But even people who follow Jesus get distracted.

We are prone to get sidetracked by momentary interests. Our eyes drift from Jesus and fix themselves on other leaders. We look back to the past and remember leaders from history and believe those people had it better back then. And so Hebrews asks us to consider Jesus again and again.

No matter how long you've followed Jesus, you need to consider Him again.

Hebrews directs that consideration by way of comparison. Moses was seen as the pinnacle of faithfulness in the Old Testament. He heard from God, served God well, and led others to do the same. But the point of Moses's faithfulness was to point to the superior faithfulness of Jesus Christ.

No leader, however gifted, can outmatch what Jesus accomplished. Moses was a godly man, but Jesus is God in human flesh. Moses was a servant, but Jesus is the Son. He owns the house and provides everything needed in it—that is, everything needed for us, who stand as God's household servants alongside Moses.

Considering Jesus in the way the author of Hebrews is encouraging us to do will guide us to see that nothing and no one is worth comparing to Jesus.

We might get distracted along the way. We all have people and leaders we look to, but when we consider Jesus for who He really is, our eyes will quickly shift back to Him. Jesus is beyond comparison. He is uniquely qualified to lead us to God.

The rest of this week, we'll consider the ways Jesus leads us.

Hebrews encourages you to
consider Jesus again and again.

REFLECTIONS

The message of the letter to the Hebrews could be summarized in the words, "Consider Jesus." What does it mean to consider something? What is the author of Hebrews asking us to do?

Who is a spiritual leader you admire and lean on? Why is Jesus better? Why is it important to remember this?

"Consider Jesus" in the CSB is translated "fix your thoughts on Jesus" in the NIV and "think carefully about this Jesus" in the NLT. What are some practical ways you can do this?

Jesus is better than ...

The writer of Hebrews consistently uses the Greek word *kreitton*, which means "more excellent," "superior," or "better." There are many faithful leaders recorded in Scripture, but all of these leaders were meant to point us to the superiority of Jesus. We can certainly learn moral lessons from them, but beyond moral lessons we need to see how each of these characters point to Jesus and teach us about who He is.

... Abraham.

John 8:53-58

... David.

Matthew 9:27
2 Samuel 7:16
Psalm 110:1
Matthew 22:45

... John the Baptist.

Luke 7:26-28
Malachi 3:1
Luke 1:17
Mark 1:7-8

... Jacob.

Genesis 32:28
John 4:10-14

... Solomon.

1 Kings 10:23-24
Matthew 12:42

... the church.

Ephesians 5:27
Colossians 1:18
John 13:16

... Moses.

Exodus 33:11
Deuteronomy 18:15
Matthew 5:17
Romans 8:2
Hebrews 3:3

... Jonah.

Jonah 3
Matthew 12:41

... all other names.

Philippians 2:9
Acts 4:12

HEBREWS 4:12-13

[12] For the word of God is living and effective and sharper than any double-edged sword, penetrating as far as the separation of soul and spirit, joints and marrow. It is able to judge the thoughts and intentions of the heart. [13] No creature is hidden from him, but all things are naked and exposed to the eyes of him to whom we must give an account.

REVEALER AND HEALER

Most book retailers sell self-help or self improvement books. These books operate on a formula. They include some mixture of humor, motivational advice, memorable stories, and novel insights. We like authors that package their advice in short, digestible chapters—ones that don't ask or require much of us. We want to be changed without being challenged.

Many people approach the Bible in the same way, but from inside the pages of the Bible the author of Hebrews describes its content in a very different way. He wrote that the words of the Bible are "sharper than a double-edged sword." They pierce us in the deepest places of our thoughts and hearts. They lay us naked and exposed to God who holds us accountable for what He finds.

Scripture also expresses itself as a mirror, a hammer, and a lamp (James 1:23-25; Jeremiah 23:29; Psalm 119:105). These analogies make us more than a little bit uncomfortable. We want to mold the Bible into our image, like a selfie, where we can use filters and crop tools to ignore our imperfections and feel good about what we have deemed our "best" selves. But the Bible doesn't work like that. It shows us who we are and where we need to make changes by penetrating and judging the heart, breaking apart our hard places, and illuminating the way we should go.

That way is Jesus. The Bible is how we come to know Him because it is where He is most fully revealed. Jesus is the personification of the written and spoken Word (see John 1:1). He came to earth to communicate and reveal God to the world.

The Bible has unique power to dissect and heal our deepest issues because it is a book written to us and for us by our Creator. The Bible reveals our hidden sin and faults and leads us to find healing in Jesus.

The Scriptures invite us to look to Jesus and follow His leading as we become more like Him and embrace a life that reflects our Creator's purposes for us.

The Scriptures show you who God is,
and who you are.

REFLECTIONS

Look over the verses again. How are the Scriptures described?

What are some areas of your life that you have been trying to hide from God? How does God's Word speak into those issues?

How has God used the Scriptures to lead you? What is an area of life where you need them to lead you now?

HEBREWS 4:14-16

OUR GREAT HIGH PRIEST

[14] Therefore, since we have a great high priest who has passed through the heavens — Jesus the Son of God — let us hold fast to our confession. [15] For we do not have a high priest who is unable to sympathize with our weaknesses, but one who has been tempted in every way as we are, yet without sin. [16] Therefore, let us approach the throne of grace with boldness, so that we may receive mercy and find grace to help us in time of need.

HELPER AND MEDIATOR

Sometimes when you share a difficulty or struggle with a friend, they immediately start telling you about one of their own. They're not meaning to one-up you or minimize your situation; they're just trying to relate. It's a peculiar tendency and largely unhelpful, but the misguided intention in their self-focus is to offer some sort of sympathetic help.

Jesus is not like your well-meaning, yet unhelpful friend. He doesn't interrupt so He can interject, He listens and affirms. He understands.

In the Old Testament, the high priest represented God to people and people to God (more on this on the following page). Jesus does both more intentionally and fully than any priest ever could. He is truly man and truly God and contains both perspectives in one person.

Jesus doesn't look at our need from the outside, caring about us but still personally removed from our struggles and unable to identify with them. He doesn't attempt to relate to our struggle. He actually does relate to us in the very best possible way.

Jesus's sympathy is not limited to feelings; it always includes His active help because of His presence within us. He chose, and still chooses, to join us in our struggle. And now He advocates for us in our suffering from the throne room of heaven. He provides the help that no one else can.

Because God is holy (which is to say morally perfect) we need more than a helper. We need a mediator to bring us into the throne room of heaven and give us access to God. Because Jesus is our High Priest we can approach God with boldness and can turn to God in confident prayer knowing that He will hear and answer us.

Jesus does not sit far off, nodding His head as if to say, "Yeah, I've been there. That's a tough one." As our Great High Priest, He understands what we're going through even better than we do, steps into it with us, and provides the way out.

Jesus relates to our struggle as our Helper and Mediator.

REFLECTIONS

According to these verses, describe the access we have to God the Father because of Jesus.

Where do you need Jesus to be your helper and mediator?

Write Hebrews 4:15 on a note card and work to memorize it. Name a hurt or hardship you're struggling to get past. How does Hebrews 4:15 encourage you in that temptation?

INSIGHTS

In the Old Testament system, the high priest was the head of the Sanhedrin, or supreme court. His role was to make sacrifices to God for the Hebrew people so they would remain in right relationship with God. To do that, the high priest had to make great preparations to enter the most holy place in the tabernacle once a year (Leviticus 16).

Though He is God, Jesus chose to become our great high priest. To do this, He had to become completely human and live a sinless life so that He could provide Himself as the once-and-for-all needed sacrifice for our sins. Jesus's life, death, and resurrection emphasize the depth of God's mercy in determining to identify with us.

HEBREWS 5:1-10

5 For every high priest taken from among men is appointed in matters pertaining to God for the people, to offer both gifts and sacrifices for sins. [2] He is able to deal gently with those who are ignorant and are going astray, since he is also clothed with weakness. [3] Because of this, he must make an offering for his own sins as well as for the people. [4] No one takes this honor on himself; instead, a person is called by God, just as Aaron was. [5] In the same way, Christ did not exalt himself to become a high priest, but God who said to him,

> **You are my Son;**
>
> **today I have become your Father,**

[6] also says in another place,

> **You are a priest forever**
>
> **according to the order of Melchizedek.**

[7] During his earthly life, he offered prayers and appeals with loud cries and tears to the one who was able to save him from death, and he was heard because of his reverence. [8] Although he was the Son, he learned obedience from what he suffered. [9] After he was perfected, he became the source of eternal salvation for all who obey him, [10] and he was declared by God a high priest according to the order of Melchizedek.

PRIEST AND KING

As we read through Hebrews, we might be tempted to move quickly past chapter 5, confused about why we need to learn about a guy with a hard to pronounce name who was a priest and a king thousands of years ago. But the writer of Hebrews thought it was important for us to meet Melchizedek—so important that he devoted an entire chapter explaining why (Hebrews 7).

Like every other example in the book of Hebrews, Melchizedek is included because he teaches us important truths about Jesus.

First, we must understand that Aaron (the brother of Moses) was the original high priest. Like all other human high priests after him, he was asked by God to serve in this way. Like all other human priests, Aaron sinned, so in the sacrificial system of the Old Testament, he had to make offerings for himself as well as the people.

Jesus is a different type of high priest. To help us understand that, the writer of Hebrews called attention to Melchizedek, who is only mentioned twice in the Old Testament (Genesis 14:18 and Psalm 110:4). Melchizedek was both a king and a priest. Aside from this, we know very little about Melchizedek's life. We know nothing of his ancestry or death. He also predates Aaron so he's a different kind of priest than Aaron. Melchizedek is in the Bible because he serves as a symbol of the priesthood of Christ.

Jesus was, and is, better than any priest who came before or after Him. He is a priest and a king, with no beginning and no end. He took the titles of priest and king to a new level by being the sinless Son of God. He didn't need to offer a sacrifice for His sins, because He never sinned.

We are covered in weakness, and there's nothing we or any human priest can do to change that. Our only hope is Jesus, who God appointed to stand as the perfect high priest on our behalf to sympathize with us and provide the perfect sacrifice for our sins.

Jesus is a perfect priest and king.

REFLECTIONS

Based on these verses, how is Jesus a better high priest than any other high priest?

When has God used an imperfect leader to reveal to you your need for the perfect Jesus?

What would it mean for you to lay down your feeble attempts at covering your own sin and weakness and embrace Jesus as your covering? Have you done that? How do you know?

INSIGHTS

Melchizedek is only mentioned twice in the Old Testament (Genesis 14:18 and Psalm 110:4). He is the first person in the Bible to be referred to as a priest. His name means "king of righteousness" and "King of Salem" which means "King of Peace." These are titles that also apply to Jesus. It is clear from Genesis that Abraham understood Melchizedek to be a priest of Yahweh, the God of the Bible.

Offices of Jesus

One of the contributions that Hebrews makes to the story of Scripture is the way it describes what theologians call the "Offices of Christ" which describe the work Jesus does or the role He occupies. In Hebrews, these offices are prophet, priest, and king.[1]

PROPHET

Jesus is an apostle who prophetically announced the kingdom of God.

> **HEBREWS 3:1** Therefore, holy brothers and sisters, who share in a heavenly calling, consider Jesus, the apostle and high priest of our confession.

Additionally, the book of Acts confirms that Jesus is the prophet like Moses, promised in the Old Testament.

> **ACTS 3:22-23** Moses said: The Lord your God will raise up for you a prophet like me from among your brothers. You must listen to everything he tells you. And everyone who does not listen to that prophet will be completely cut off from the people.

PRIEST

He is the Great High Priest who provided the ultimate sacrifice for our sins.

> **HEBREWS 8:1** Now the main point of what is being said is this: We have this kind of high priest, who sat down at the right hand of the throne of the Majesty in the heavens.

> **HEBREWS 4:14-15** Therefore, since we have a great high priest who has passed through the heavens—Jesus the Son of God—let us hold fast to our confession. For we do not have a high priest who is unable to sympathize with our weaknesses, but one who has been tempted in every way as we are, yet without sin.

KING

Jesus is a messianic king who reigns on the throne of heaven.

> **HEBREWS 1:3** The Son is the radiance of God's glory and the exact expression of his nature, sustaining all things by his powerful word.

> **HEBREWS 2:9** But we do see Jesus—made lower than the angels for a short time so that by God's grace he might taste death for everyone—crowned with glory and honor because he suffered death.

1. J. I. Packer, *Concise Theology: A Guide to Historic Christian Beliefs* (Wheaton, IL: Tyndale House, 1993), 132–133.

HEBREWS 6:13-20

INHERITING THE PROMISE

[13] For when God made a promise to Abraham, since he had no one greater to swear by, he swore by himself: [14] **I will indeed bless you, and I will greatly multiply you.** [15] And so, after waiting patiently, Abraham obtained the promise. [16] For people swear by something greater than themselves, and for them a confirming oath ends every dispute. [17] Because God wanted to show his unchangeable purpose even more clearly to the heirs of the promise, he guaranteed it with an oath, [18] so that through two unchangeable things, in which it is impossible for God to lie, we who have fled for refuge might have strong encouragement to seize the hope set before us. [19] We have this hope as an anchor for the soul, firm and secure. It enters the inner sanctuary behind the curtain. [20] Jesus has entered there on our behalf as a forerunner, because he has become a high priest forever according to the order of Melchizedek.

FAITHFUL AND TRUE

We live in a world where it's hard to know what to believe. Every day, people make promises. And then they break them. We read and trust "news" that turns out to be fake. The struggle is so great that the global demand for positive proof has led to the popularity of multiple fact-checking organizations and websites.

God always keeps His promises. Without exception or excuse, He does what He says He will do.

To prove His faithfulness God swore an oath. Growing up, you likely heard someone "swear to God" to underscore the seriousness of their promise. Well God is basically doing that Himself. However, unlike us, God didn't need to do anything extra to make His promise legitimate or true, but He did. God swore because He knew we, like the Hebrews, would struggle with doubt and be tempted to turn away from Him. God swore because He wants us to have assurance in our hope (v. 11).

Abraham was a good example for the Hebrews because they knew the story of Abraham well, and how God kept His promises to him. And today God keeps this promise to us through the new covenant—a commitment to reconciliation and intimacy with Him—administered through Jesus.

God's past faithfulness ensures His future faithfulness.

God keeps His promises because God does not change. He was not a liar then and He is not a liar now. God is a better leader and promise-keeper, expressed rhetorically in Numbers 23:19 this way: "God is not a man, that he might lie, or a son of man, that he might change his mind. Does he speak and not act, or promise and not fulfill?"

God's faithfulness to this promise secures our future with Him. Every single blessing we receive from Jesus is dependent on better promises from God which are kept for us in Jesus.

God's faithfulness secures your future with Him.

REFLECTIONS

What purpose does an anchor serve on a boat? What does it mean for Jesus to be an anchor for our souls (v. 19)?

In what situation do you need to seize the hope of Jesus's better leadership as an anchor for your soul, firm and secure?

What changes would take place in your life this week if you were to truly believe, without question, that God will keep His promises to you in Christ?

INSIGHTS

The curtain in the temple (v. 19) separated the holy of holies from the rest of the temple area. The ark of the covenant was in the holy of holies. This box contained relics that proved their connection with God and His promises. The high priest of Israel was the only one who could pass through the curtain and enter the holy of holies. He made offerings for the sins of the people of Israel. When Jesus died on the cross making payment for the sins of humankind, the curtain ripped (Matthew 27:51-54). But it didn't rip in the hands of a human. The curtain was ripped from top to bottom, an act of God. Jesus's sacrificial death tore down the separation between us and God. We don't need someone to represent us in the holy of holies—Jesus is the leader who carries us toward maturity.

PAUSE & LISTEN

Spend some time reflecting over the week's reading.

Therefore, holy brothers and sisters, who share in a heavenly calling, consider Jesus, the apostle and high priest of our confession . . . Christ was faithful as a Son over his household. And we are that household if we hold on to our confidence and the hope in which we boast.

HEBREWS 3:1,6

DAY
14

REFLECTION

Use these questions for personal reflection or group discussion on Hebrews 3–6.

What stuck out to you most in this week's reading? What surprised you? Confused you?

What does this week's Scripture teach you about God and His character?

What does this week's Scripture teach you about humanity and our need for grace?

How does this week's Scripture point you to Jesus?

What steps of faith and obedience is God asking you to take through these Scriptures?

Close by considering Jesus as a better leader than you have ever known. He is faithful and true, ruling and reigning, leading and guiding all who have anchored their faith in His name.

WEEK 3

BETTER HOPE

Hope in certainty.

We tend to place our hope in outcomes of chance.

If I get this new job, then my future will be secure. If my lab tests return normal, then I will be content. If my romantic relationship stays healthy and strong, then my life will be complete.

The Hebrew Christians were in that kind of "If, then" state of mind. They had grabbed onto new faith in Jesus Christ, but then, over time, circumstances caused their grip to slip. They had endured persecution, but their endurance was now fading.

So they considered placing their hope in an outcome of chance. They thought turning back to Judaism might be their only hope for continuing to draw near to God.

If we choose another way of relating to God, then our lives will be better.

The writer of Hebrews wrote to remind them, and us, that if we place our hope of God in chance, we will not receive the outcome we are looking for.

A better hope is introduced, through which we draw near to God (Hebrews 7:19b).

This better hope is Jesus. This hope is not subjective. Hope in the finished work of Christ on the cross is not one of chance or uncertainty. Jesus is the only guarantee of victory.

HEBREWS 7:26-28

[26] For this is the kind of high priest we need: holy, innocent, undefiled, separated from sinners, and exalted above the heavens. [27] He doesn't need to offer sacrifices every day, as high priests do — first for their own sins, then for those of the people. He did this once for all time when he offered himself. [28] For the law appoints as high priests men who are weak, but the promise of the oath, which came after the law, appoints a Son, who has been perfected forever.

THE HERO WE NEED

Our desire to be saved is all over contemporary culture. You need not look any further than the unparalleled success of the Marvel Cinematic Universe. We love the moment when against all odds, and at great personal sacrifice, the heroes stand victorious.

Throughout those superhero stories are numerous Christological references. It's clear, we largely agree that we need someone to give up everything in order to save us. And we know that someone needs to be different than us. He or she has to have resources that we cannot tap into or else we wouldn't need to be saved.

In Hebrews, we are assured that such a Hero exists.

Like any hero, Jesus has qualities that belong only to Him. Jesus is unlike any previous priest in moral purity and qualification. He is holy, innocent, undefiled, separated from sinners, and exalted above the heavens. He doesn't need to offer sacrifices every day, because He offered the perfect sacrifice when He gave up His own life on the cross. That sacrifice saved humanity once and for all.

Jesus is not a weak man who carried out a helpful assignment to the best of his ability; He is the holy Son of God, who has now been perfected forever. And that is why Jesus is a better representative on our behalf before the throne of God.

He is not the hero we at all deserve, but He is the Hero we need. He is the only hero who can bear the weight of our hope.

Jesus is the Hero you need.

REFLECTIONS

Based on this passage, how would you describe Jesus's character?

Which of those qualities of Jesus stands out to you right now as offering the most hope? Why?

What would change if you actively believed in and pursued that hope?

TRACING THE STORY

Hebrews connects the life of Jesus Christ to Old Testament history and practices more thoroughly than any other book in the New Testament. Jesus taught that He came to fulfill the Old Testament law (Matthew 5:17-18). The author of Hebrews echoed those words by saying that the old covenant was completed in the new covenant (7:20–8:13). Hebrews also shows that because the old covenant has been fulfilled in the new covenant by the ministry of Jesus, the new covenant is "better" (7:22).

HEBREWS 8:1-6

A HEAVENLY PRIESTHOOD

8 Now the main point of what is being said is this: We have this kind of high priest, who sat down at the right hand of the throne of the Majesty in the heavens, ² a minister of the sanctuary and the true tabernacle that was set up by the Lord and not man. ³ For every high priest is appointed to offer gifts and sacrifices; therefore, it was necessary for this priest also to have something to offer. ⁴ Now if he were on earth, he wouldn't be a priest, since there are those offering the gifts prescribed by the law. ⁵ These serve as a copy and shadow of the heavenly things, as Moses was warned when he was about to complete the tabernacle. For God said, **Be careful that you make everything according to the pattern that was shown to you on the mountain.** ⁶ But Jesus has now obtained a superior ministry, and to that degree he is the mediator of a better covenant, which has been established on better promises.

REAL HOPE

Hebrews chapter 8 serves as a hinge in the book. The point of the letter hinges on the truth of this section where the writer makes the case that everything else in the Bible points to Jesus. In other words, He is the point of it all. Everyone and everything else is just a "copy and shadow."

The Old Testament tabernacle and temple were only a copy and shadow, an incomplete picture of the reality of experiencing God's presence through Jesus. God gave great detail for their construction so that they would reflect, but not replace, the greater reality to come. The priesthood was also only a copy and shadow, an incomplete picture, of the priestly role Jesus fulfills for us in heaven. The animal sacrifices were only a copy and shadow, an incomplete picture, of the once-and-for-all sacrifice of Christ on the cross for us.

As you consider Jesus, consider this: He sits at the right hand of the throne of God in Heaven. This is the kind of high priest He is. He is not a copy and shadow of anything or anyone greater. He is entirely different. He sits where no other priest could ever sit and He does what no other priest could ever do.

Jesus is a better Mediator, perfectly and forever representing sinful people before a holy God. Jesus has established a better covenant, perfectly and forever fulfilling the requirement of the law on our behalf. Jesus enacts that covenant through better promises, perfectly enduring throughout all eternity.

While there are many things—even good things—we might be tempted to place our hope in, there is no better hope than Jesus. Every other hope is only a copy and shadow of what we find in Jesus.

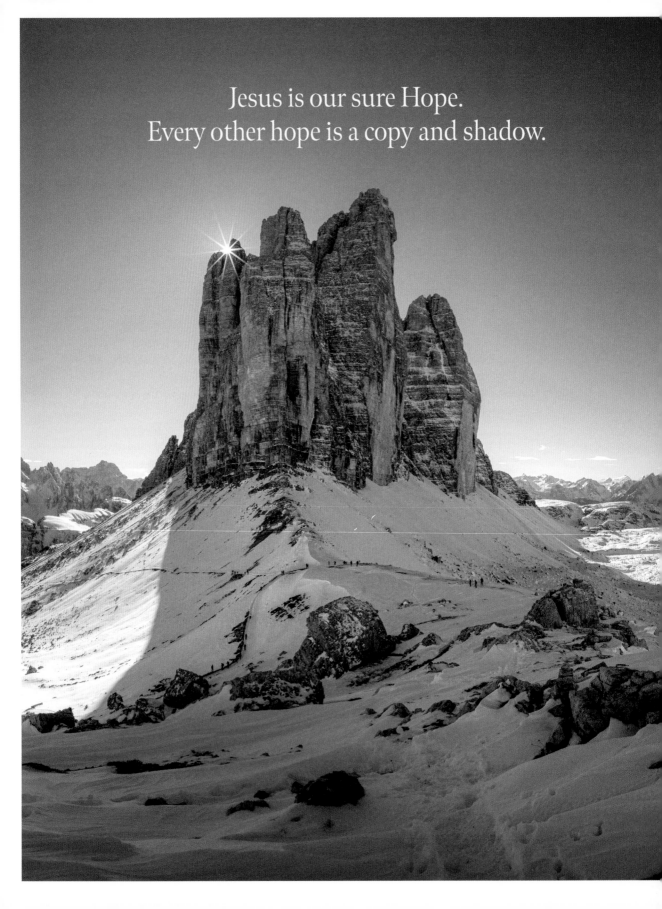

Jesus is our sure Hope.
Every other hope is a copy and shadow.

REFLECTIONS

What are some things today that serve as a copy and shadow of real hope in Christ?

How can you guard against prioritizing those things above the reality of Christ's ministry in your life?

Are you looking for something new from God? How can you remind yourself, in every circumstance and season, of the fullness of the hope He's already given to you in Jesus?

INSIGHTS

The author of Hebrews frequently uses a lesser to greater argument. For example, the temple and the sacrifices of the old covenant are a lesser version of the greater Christ. The words "copy" and "shadow" help us understand what he means. Consider a photocopy: it looks close enough to the real thing, but it's also clear that it's not the best version of the document. The same can be said for a shadow. It gives you a sense of an object, but distorts the edges and perspective. The old covenant is only a copy and shadow of what we have been given in Jesus.

HEBREWS 9:11-14

NEW COVENANT MINISTRY

[11] But Christ has appeared as a high priest of the good things that have come. In the greater and more perfect tabernacle not made with hands (that is, not of this creation), [12] he entered the most holy place once for all time, not by the blood of goats and calves, but by his own blood, having obtained eternal redemption. [13] For if the blood of goats and bulls and the ashes of a young cow, sprinkling those who are defiled, sanctify for the purification of the flesh, [14] how much more will the blood of Christ, who through the eternal Spirit offered himself without blemish to God, cleanse our consciences from dead works so that we can serve the living God?

FREE

Some start out on a career path with hopes of doing good in the world. Others start out with hopes of making as much money as possible. And it's not uncommon for people in both categories to become jaded at some point along the way. We begin to view our jobs as a means to a less grandiose end, often simply expressed this way—"It pays the bills."

The same thing happens when we set our hopes on our own abilities and efforts to do good and make the most impact. It wears us down, especially when we realize we actually can't pay the bill we owe. The debt of our sin is too great for any amount of good works to cover.

This was exactly the case under the old covenant. The Law required constant sacrifice to "pay" for sin. The people had to do good works, but their work was never good enough, and the priests had to regularly enter the tabernacle, offering animal sacrifices to pay down the debt that sin accumulated and restore fellowship with God.

Then Jesus did the work no one else could possibly do. He entered where no one else could, and provided a once-and-for-all-time sacrifice that frees us from the insufficient hope of our own abilities and efforts.

Jesus paid your debt in full.

His blood sacrifice restores our relationship to God. And it frees us up to live a better way. In Him, life and work have new and profound meaning. We don't work to pay the debt we owe, we work to joyfully serve the living God.

Jesus's sacrifice frees you from the insufficient hope of your own abilities and efforts.

REFLECTIONS

Why is a cleansed conscience important (v. 14)?

Is there any area of life in which you need a clear conscience? How does the condition of your conscience affect the way you serve God?

What are some ways you have tried to pay for your own sin? What does it look like to work for what Christ has already achieved for you?

HEBREWS 10:1-4

THE PERFECT SACRIFICE

10 Since the law has only a shadow of the good things to come, and not the reality itself of those things, it can never perfect the worshipers by the same sacrifices they continually offer year after year. ² Otherwise, wouldn't they have stopped being offered, since the worshipers, purified once and for all, would no longer have any consciousness of sins? ³ But in the sacrifices there is a reminder of sins year after year. ⁴ For it is impossible for the blood of bulls and goats to take away sins.

ONCE FOR ALL

The saying goes, "If at first you don't succeed, try, try again."

The origin of that phrase is attributed to an educator named Thomas H. Palmer in 1840. He said it as way of encouraging children to do their homework.[1] However, we can safely assume that Hebrew grown-ups understood that same truth thousands of years before.

Spiritually speaking, failure was part of the eventual victory, right from the start.

It wasn't that God's first plan failed and He had to start over again and try something new. Rather, "step one"—the law, was ultimately instated to point us to and prepare us for Jesus. In the law, the sacrifices and rituals had to be performed over and over again. The old covenant was only the first step and had been such all along. God was not really seeking any type of animal sacrifice. Killing animals couldn't kill sin's effect.

Jesus came and taught that spiritual health can never be achieved from "try, try again."

Jesus, the Messiah, came as a far better step two—not continuous incomplete sacrifices and offerings, because God didn't want that anyway. Instead, a person devoted to continuously and perfectly fulfilling God's will, offering a once-for-all complete and final sacrifice.

Many of us place our hope in what we do. These hopes are feeble and only last until our next shortcoming or failure. Jesus made one sacrifice that frees all who trust in Him from needing any other sacrifices. In Jesus, we are free from the up and down, we are accepted once and for all time because of His work on our behalf.

1."Well-Known Expressions: If at first you don't succeed, try, try again," Book Browse, BookBrowse LLC, accessed April 28, 2022, https://www.bookbrowse.com/expressions/detail/index.cfm/ expression_number/586/if-at-first-you-dont-succeed-try-try-again.

Spiritual success doesn't come from your best attempts to "try, try again."

REFLECTIONS

When have you felt like your trying to do and be good has failed you?

If the Law and continuous sacrifices could never perfect us, then why did God require them? What was God really looking for in the sacrifices of the old covenant?

What are some "sacrifices" people today make again and again in an attempt to please God? What does Hebrews 10:1-4 teach you about those efforts?

Jesus and the New Covenant

Hebrews continually utilizes Old Testament history to show that Jesus and the new covenant are better. The old covenant requires repeated sacrifice to maintain personal holiness and fellowship with God. In the new covenant each of these aspects is fulfilled in Jesus. They are no longer necessary. Jesus said it best:

> Don't think that I came to abolish the Law or the Prophets. I did not come to abolish but to fulfill. For truly I tell you, until heaven and earth pass away, not the smallest letter or one stroke of a letter will pass away from the law until all things are accomplished.
>
> **MATTHEW 5:17-18**

SIN

HEBREWS 7:26; 1 JOHN 3:5	EXODUS 32:21-25; LEVITICUS 4:3
Jesus the Great High Priest never sinned.	Old Testament priests sinned and God made provision for those sins.

THE TABERNACLE

HEBREWS 8:2; 9:11,24	EXODUS 25:40; 33:7
The true tabernacle where Jesus serves was set up by God in heaven.	The tabernacle where earthly priests served was set up by men as a reflection of the heavenly tabernacle.

ATONEMENT

HEBREWS 9:13-14	LEVITICUS 16:14-15; NUMBERS 19:2,9,17-18
Jesus's blood forever and completely cleanses us from all sin.	Old Testament rituals of sacrifice were continually done for the purification of sins.

SACRIFICE

HEBREWS 10:5-8	PSALM 40:6-8
Because God did not want animal sacrifices, Jesus came to do God's will.	David foretold Christ's mission to do God's will by offering a better sacrifice.

HEBREWS 10:5-10

⁵ Therefore, as he was coming into the world, he said:

> You did not desire sacrifice and offering,
>
> but you prepared a body for me.
>
> ⁶ You did not delight
>
> in whole burnt offerings and sin offerings.
>
> ⁷ Then I said, "See—
>
> it is written about me
>
> in the scroll—
>
> I have come to do your will, God."

⁸ After he says above, **You did not desire or delight in sacrifices and offerings, whole burnt offerings and sin offerings** (which are offered according to the law), ⁹ he then says, **See, I have come to do your will.** He takes away the first to establish the second. ¹⁰ By this will, we have been sanctified through the offering of the body of Jesus Christ once for all time.

THE WORK IS COMPLETE

There's something satisfying about the completion of a project. Likewise there is something frustrating about a project we can never finish.

When our work remains undone, it frustrates us and makes moving forward difficult. We think, "My work is never done!" and that knowledge is paralyzing.

Many of us import this same line of thinking into our spiritual lives. We often live as though there is still more to be done if we are to truly find God's favor. We live as if that undone work is our responsibility. We don't trust that what Jesus did was enough.

That kind of thinking is ultimately hopeless. For thousands of years, long before us, people tried to fulfill that responsibility and couldn't do it. Because it's an impossible task for any person who has ever once sinned.

But Jesus never sinned. His perfect obedience and death completely fulfilled the will of God. Not partly. *Completely.* Jesus's life, death, and resurrection didn't take care of some things we need. He took care of everything.

When we trust in Jesus, we are supernaturally identified with Him. When we are identified with Him, we also have, again supernaturally, fulfilled the will of God.

In Christ, you have fulfilled the will of God. There is nothing left to do!

No work is undone; no sacrifice remains. Jesus replaced the sacrificial system. Because of Him, our hope extends beyond the most recent sacrifice. God receives us on the basis of the fact that Jesus did everything God required of us. Because of Jesus God is perfectly pleased with us. Nothing else is needed! This is why the writer of Hebrews wrote, "Once for all time." The work is complete.

Jesus's life, death, and resurrection didn't only take care of some things you need. He took care of everything.

REFLECTIONS

What are some things we do in an attempt to make amends with God?

What are some signs you are resting in the completed work of Christ on your behalf? What are some signs you're still taking on that responsibility yourself?

What are some steps you can take to daily remember the completeness of Jesus's work to free you from sin's death grip?

PAUSE & LISTEN

Spend some time reflecting over the week's reading.

For the law perfected nothing,
but a better hope is
introduced, through which
we draw near to God.

HEBREWS 7:19

REFLECTION

Use these questions for personal reflection or group discussion on Hebrews 7:26–10:10.

What stuck out to you most in this week's reading? What surprised you? Confused you?

What does this week's Scripture teach you about God and His character?

What does this week's Scripture teach you about humanity and our need for grace?

How does this week's Scripture point you to Jesus?

What steps of faith and obedience is God asking you to take through these Scriptures?

PRAY

Rest in the hope we have in Jesus. Pray that knowing Jesus would free you from placing your hope in anything else. Embrace His work for you and believe in Him.

WEEK 4

BETTER ACCESS

Access God through faith in Jesus.

Before turning in faith to Jesus, these Hebrew believers had, in effect, been taking piggyback rides to get to God. They were approaching God through mediators.

The priests purified themselves for the purpose of entering God's presence and offering sacrifices to make atonement for many. By proxy, one holy man was given audience with the Lord one day out of the year, on behalf of the masses. But when Jesus made one final sacrifice, He fulfilled and abolished the role of the priest.

They couldn't piggyback into God's presence anymore. Jesus had made it so that they didn't need to. Now every person had access to God. They could enter into God's presence themselves through their own faith.

The message of Hebrews 10 and 11 is that Jesus had given them everything they needed to do that—to own their faith. He had given them new hearts, personal holiness, and had drawn them to Himself and each other.

These gifts were theirs no matter what circumstances they might face. But they each had to take some responsibility if they wanted to see the fulfillment of those promises play out in their lives.

And so do we.

HEBREWS 10:11-18

[11] Every priest stands day after day ministering and offering the same sacrifices time after time, which can never take away sins. [12] But this man, after offering one sacrifice for sins forever, sat down at the right hand of God. [13] He is now waiting until his enemies are made his footstool. [14] For by one offering he has perfected forever those who are sanctified. [15] The Holy Spirit also testifies to us about this. For after he says:

[16] **This is the covenant I will make with them**

    after those days,

the Lord says,

    I will put my laws on their hearts

    and write them on their minds,

[17] and **I will never again remember**

    their sins and their lawless acts.

[18] Now where there is forgiveness of these, there is no longer an offering for sin.

<table>
<tr><td>DAY
22</td><td># A NEW HEART</td></tr>
</table>

In a difficult circumstance, you may have heard someone reflect, "I don't know how people do this without Jesus." In the face of war, pandemic, personal loss, injustice, and death, there is grief for every person. So it is mind-boggling for those who know Jesus to consider what it might be like to face those things without Him.

It seems the writer of Hebrews had similar thoughts. In explaining the permanence of Jesus's sacrifice and forgiveness of sins, the writer pointed back again to the Old Testament, quoting words that had been given to the people of Israel by the prophet Jeremiah (31:33-34). At that time, the Babylonians were breathing down their necks, and they faced imminent exile.

As it was for these Hebrew Christians, life was hard.

The difference, though, was that the people in Jeremiah's day were under the old covenant. They had the law, annual sacrifices, priests to perform them, and a prophet to speak to them on God's behalf. They also had the promise of the new covenant. But it hadn't come yet.

In recalling that promise, which *was* now fulfilled for them in Jesus, it is as if the writer of Hebrews was saying, "They had to do this without Jesus, but you do not!"

Jesus has given us the fullness of what we saw the dim hope of in the priest. Jesus gives us better access to God because God's law is written on our hearts. Because of Jesus, in whatever circumstances we face, God is constantly orienting our hearts toward Him.

In times of struggle and hardship, we have the ability to go directly to the source of comfort and peace through our new hearts that are connected to His. We never struggle alone, we're always connect to Him.

Jesus gives you better access to God
because He gives you a new heart.

REFLECTIONS

How does the new heart Jesus gives you change the way you relate to God?

In what situation are you struggling to experience the reality of the new heart you have received?

Even when God's law is written on our hearts and minds, we are still prone to sin. How can we continue to orient our hearts and lives toward God, even when our flesh is drawn away?

INSIGHTS

The Greek word *hagiazo* is used twenty-eight times in the New Testament, and is translated into different English words because it conveys several different shades of meaning. In Hebrews 10:14, *hagiazo* is translated as "sanctified," and indicates the dedication of a person in holy service to God.

HEBREWS 10:19-23

EXHORTATIONS TO GODLINESS

[19] Therefore, brothers and sisters, since we have boldness to enter the sanctuary through the blood of Jesus — [20] he has inaugurated for us a new and living way through the curtain (that is, through his flesh) — [21] and since we have a great high priest over the house of God, [22] let us draw near with a true heart in full assurance of faith, with our hearts sprinkled clean from an evil conscience and our bodies washed in pure water. [23] Let us hold on to the confession of our hope without wavering, since he who promised is faithful.

A NEW WAY

Have you ever taken a tour of the White House? It's not a complicated process getting in on that deal. You simply submit your request, wait for instructions, and then show up at the appointed time with your government-issued photo identification. But you should have zero confidence that you will see the President, the Oval Office, or any other part of the West Wing, for that matter. White House tours are limited to the museum-like rooms in the East Wing. To try to go anywhere else outside of that carefully chosen path would not end your D.C. vacation well!

Before Jesus died on the cross, getting into God's inner sanctuary in the temple, the holy of holies, required more vetting than getting into the Oval Office to see the president. Everyone could enter the courtyard, but only chosen priests were allowed into the sanctuary. And only the High Priest, once a year on the Day of Atonement, could go into the holy of holies. He didn't just wake up and walk in, either. There were very specific instructions about everything surrounding that event, including what clothes he needed to wear and what sacrifices he had to make.

For a Hebrew having grown up under those laws, it would have been absolutely mind-blowing to consider that Jesus gives every person freedom to enter into the sanctuary of God's holy presence, and the confidence to do it.

Access to God had been blocked by sin. It had been that way throughout their history with God. But the writer of Hebrews reminds these Jewish believers, and us today, that Jesus made a better way.

Jesus has drawn us to Himself and to each other through His sacrifice on our behalf.

Each of us tries to get access to God in a number of ways. We believe if we're good enough or if we've done enough we can gain access, but the truth is the only one who has done enough is Jesus and everything He did, He did to secure access to God for those who place their faith in Him. That's why Jesus's way is a "new and living way" (v. 20).

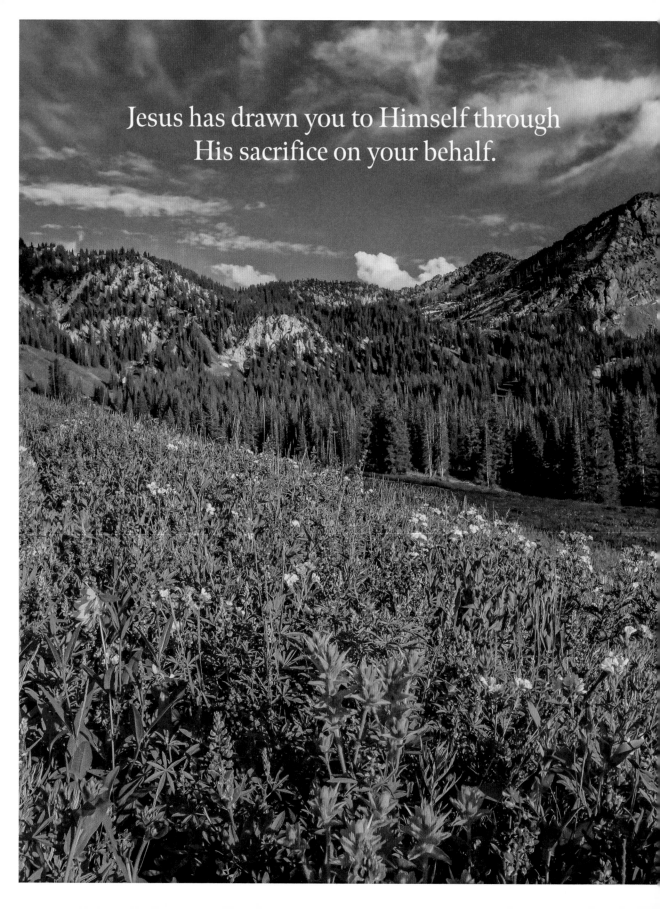

Jesus has drawn you to Himself through
His sacrifice on your behalf.

REFLECTIONS

Reread the words of verse 23. What does it mean to you to read that when Jesus makes a promise, He is always faithful?

In difficult times, how does knowing that you can draw near to God help you hold on?

What does it mean for you to enter God's presence with "boldness"? What is a situation in your life about which you need to do that?

INSIGHTS

If the high priest did not enter the most holy place exactly according to the prescribed instructions he was given, he could die on the spot (Leviticus 16:2). Those very explicit instructions are given in Leviticus 16:2-34 and Hebrews 9:6-7.

HEBREWS 10:26-29

WARNING AGAINST DELIBERATE SIN

[26] For if we deliberately go on sinning after receiving the knowledge of the truth, there no longer remains a sacrifice for sins, [27] but a terrifying expectation of judgment and the fury of a fire about to consume the adversaries. [28] Anyone who disregarded the law of Moses died without mercy, based on the testimony of two or three witnesses. [29] How much worse punishment do you think one will deserve who has trampled on the Son of God, who has regarded as profane the blood of the covenant by which he was sanctified, and who has insulted the Spirit of grace?

A REQUIRED RESPONSE

Have you ever been told something you would rather not know, or seen something you would rather not have seen?

Once we see the truth, we can't unsee it. We can't unknow it. We can feign ignorance, but that knowledge stays with us. As such, it demands a response, whether internal or external. Knowledge of the truth leads to a response to the truth—whether that response is embracing or rejecting it.

Jesus gives access to personal holiness. Because of Jesus we can progress in our relationship with God. These Hebrew Christians knew the truth. They knew that Jesus is better than anything sin could promise. They could pretend to not know the truth and return to the faith of their past—but it could not deliver what Christ could.

Knowledge of the truth also makes us accountable for the truth.

If we confess our sins and follow Jesus, our sins are forgiven. To deliberately keep on sinning, then, is an insult to that confession. It is an insult to God's grace in Jesus Christ. It is an insult to the better access to God that Jesus provides. This is why the writer confronts us by saying we will be held accountable for such behavior. To know Jesus and continue to sin is to deny Jesus.

Of course we will all struggle with sin this side of heaven, but how we respond to that struggle is key. This warning against sin in Hebrews is also an invitation to pursue Jesus instead. He gives something far better than what sin offers.

In our human nature we are sinful and weak, but Jesus gives us everything we need to pursue God's heart instead of our own desires. He gives us everything we need to turn from sin and follow Him.

Knowledge of the truth leads to
accountability to the truth.

REFLECTIONS

Why does the author of Hebrews take such a severe tone against sin in these verses?

What are some sins you are tempted to willfully choose, even knowing the consequences?

What changes would take place in your life this week if you were to be truly accountable in your relationship with Jesus?

HEBREWS 11:1

LIVING BY FAITH

11 Now faith is the reality of what is hoped for, the proof of what is not seen.

A FAITH REALITY

How would you define faith?

Oxford Languages gives multiple definitions:

> "Complete trust or confidence in someone or something."
> "Strong belief in God or in the doctrines of a religion,
>   based on the spiritual apprehension rather than proof."
> "A system of religious belief."
> "A strongly held belief or theory."

Those definitions can apply to many different subjects. The Bible defines faith in a much more direct way in Hebrews 11.

Like the Hebrew Christians, we are tempted to place our faith in "someone or something" besides Jesus. We hope to gain access to God through various means, but the reality is this—Jesus is the one and only way (Hebrews 10:37-39). Our hope for God can never be realized apart from faith in Jesus.

Faith in Jesus grants access to God, not good behavior or angels or priests or Moses or rules or godly leaders or going to church or best-selling books that provide spiritual advice and tips. Not well-known religions teachers like Buddha or Gandhi or Joseph Smith or L. Ron Hubbard. Not crystals or reiki or dreams or oracles. Many people promise what only faith in Jesus can deliver. To expect access to God through anything else is a fool's errand.

Faith in Jesus is the only necessity to access God.

This faith—believing in Jesus and committing our lives to Him alone—is what links us with our Creator and makes our relationship with Him an experienced reality. Faith in Jesus proves what we hope for but cannot yet see.

Faith in Jesus links you to your Creator.

REFLECTIONS

How do you think most people define the word "faith"?

Has there ever been a time in your life when any "closeness" to God you experienced was dependent on someone or something besides Jesus Himself?

Why isn't it enough to live your spiritual life vicariously through another person's access to God? How would you describe what it means to "own" your faith in Jesus?

Stories of Faith

Hebrews 11 summarizes the faith stories of numerous men
and women from Old Testament scriptures. Again, each of
these men and women are included to point us to Jesus.

ABEL

HEBREWS 11:4

God accepted Abel's offering because it was given in faith.

GENESIS 4:4

Abel brought fat portions from some of the firstborn of his flock.

ENOCH

HEBREWS 11:5

God took Enoch to heaven because Enoch lived by faith.

GENESIS 5:22-24

Enoch walked with God for 365 years.

NOAH

HEBREWS 11:7

Fear of God led Noah to obey God and rescue his family from the flood.

GENESIS 6-9

God spared Noah because he was a righteous man.

ABRAHAM & SARAH

HEBREWS 11:8-12

God gave Abraham and Sarah a child and the promise of a future inheritance that would extend to countless people because they followed Him in faith.

GENESIS 12:4

At seventy-five years of age, Abram left home with Sarai and went where the Lord told him to go.

GENESIS 21:6-7

At ninety years of age, Sarah gave birth to Isaac and found joy in the Lord's promise.

HEBREWS 11:2-12

[2] For by this our ancestors were approved.

[3] By faith we understand that the universe was created by the word of God, so that what is seen was made from things that are not visible.

[4] By faith Abel offered to God a better sacrifice than Cain did. By faith he was approved as a righteous man, because God approved his gifts, and even though he is dead, he still speaks through his faith.

[5] By faith Enoch was taken away, and so he did not experience death. **He was not to be found because God took him away.** For before he was taken away, he was approved as one who pleased God. [6] Now without faith it is impossible to please God, since the one who draws near to him must believe that he exists and that he rewards those who seek him.

[7] By faith Noah, after he was warned about what was not yet seen and motivated by godly fear, built an ark to deliver his family. By faith he condemned the world and became an heir of the righteousness that comes by faith.

[8] By faith Abraham, when he was called, obeyed and set out for a place that he was going to receive as an inheritance. He went out, even though he did not know where he was going. [9] By faith he stayed as a foreigner in the land of promise, living in tents as did Isaac and Jacob, coheirs of the same promise. [10] For he was looking forward to the city that has foundations, whose architect and builder is God.

[11] By faith even Sarah herself, when she was unable to have children, received power to conceive offspring, even though she was past the age, since she considered that the one who had promised was faithful. [12] Therefore, from one man — in fact, from one as good as dead — came offspring as numerous as the stars of the sky and as innumerable as the grains of sand along the seashore.

A HEROIC BELIEF

If you were to give chapter 11 of Hebrews a title, it would probably be, "Heroes of the Faith." In fact, you may have heard it referred to that way. That's because the whole chapter is devoted to recounting the heroic faith of men and women who have gone before us.

Their stories are diverse. As you read through the chapter you find a wide range of experiences that demonstrate faith. But the common denominator in them all is the object of their faith.

We are right to call these men and women heroes, but not because of who they were or even what they did; they are heroes because of who they placed their faith in.

Their stories show us that faith is the fulfillment of all of God's promises.

Noah didn't have the ability to bring about God's promise to deliver his family from destruction. Abraham didn't have the ability to bring about God's promise to bless all people on the earth. Sarah didn't have the ability to bring about God's promise of covenant to many offspring and nations.

In and of themselves, they had absolutely no power to do these heroic things. But they had faith in the One who did; they had faith in the One who would.

Their faith in God gave them access to the fulfillment of His promises. Our faith gives us access to the fulfillment of God's promises, too. And God's promises are fully revealed in His Son, Jesus. Our faith must be rooted in Him.

Hebrews 11:6 assures us there is no other way. Our stories, as diverse as those in Hebrews 11, will never please God or earn His blessings apart from faith in Jesus.

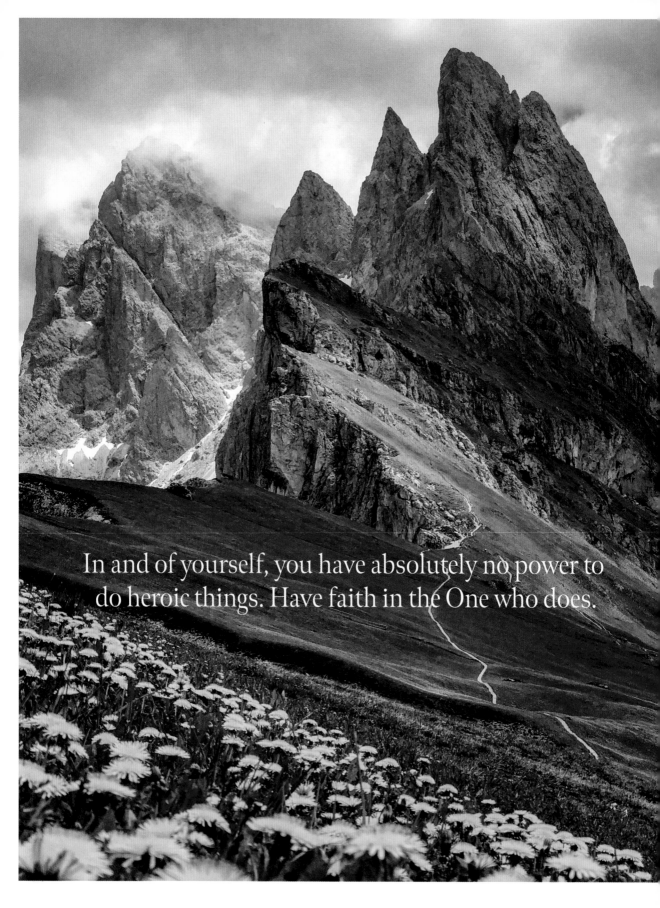

In and of yourself, you have absolutely no power to do heroic things. Have faith in the One who does.

REFLECTIONS

How did faith influence the lives and choices of the people mentioned in Hebrews 11?

What promises of God have already been fulfilled in your life? What role did your own faith in Him play?

Is there any promise of God that you're currently waiting to see fulfilled in your life? How might God be calling you to follow Him in faith in that process?

PAUSE & LISTEN

Spend some time reflecting over the week's reading.

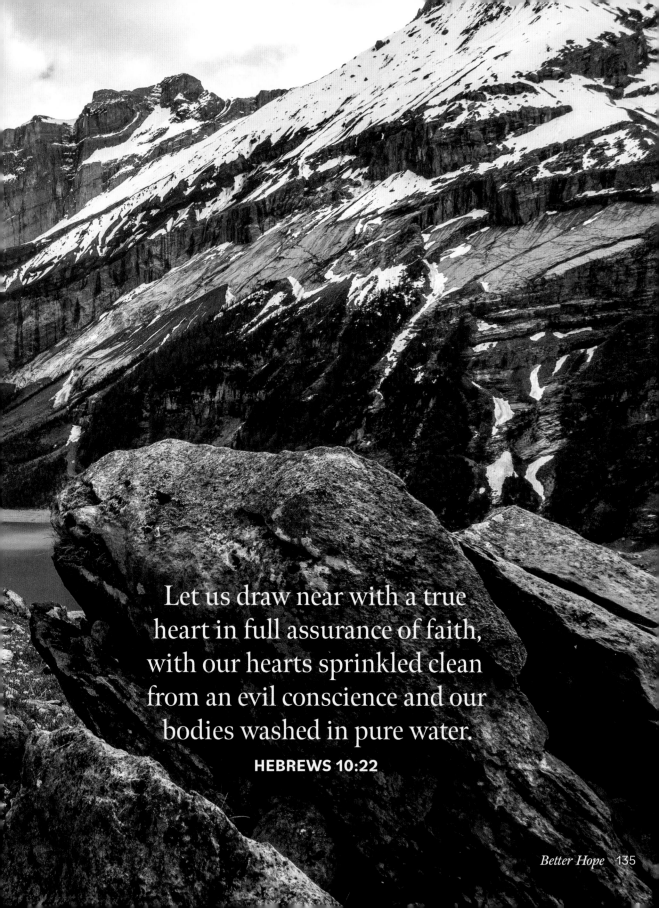

Let us draw near with a true
heart in full assurance of faith,
with our hearts sprinkled clean
from an evil conscience and our
bodies washed in pure water.

HEBREWS 10:22

REFLECTION

Use these questions for personal reflection or group discussion on Hebrews 10:11–11:12.

What stuck out to you most in this week's reading? What surprised you? Confused you?

What does this week's Scripture teach you about God and His character?

What does this week's Scripture teach you about humanity and our need for grace?

How does this week's Scripture point you to Jesus?

What steps of faith and obedience is God asking you to take through these Scriptures?

PRAY

Close thanking God for the access He has granted to us through Jesus. Pray that we would not take our faith for granted but that we would actively pursue God through a relationship with Jesus Christ.

WEEK 5

BETTER FAITH

Keep the faith.

As we saw last week, faith is a word used in different ways by people with different systems of belief.

It was the same in the first century when Hebrews was written. The Hebrew Christians had put their faith in Jesus, but like many of us today, once they had to exercise that faith in difficulty, their eyes shifted to other options.

That doesn't always happen with intention.

Sometimes we begin to place our faith in ourselves, our bank accounts, and relationships without even realizing it. It's the example we find in others around us, and we want to put our "faith" in things we can see and have some measure of control over.

Faith in Jesus is different. And it is better.

The writer of Hebrews has shown us why Jesus is superior to everything and everyone else. In chapters 11 and 12, we'll see how that truth ought to direct our faith.

HEBREWS 11:13-16

[13] These all died in faith, although they had not received the things that were promised. But they saw them from a distance, greeted them, and confessed that they were foreigners and temporary residents on the earth. [14] Now those who say such things make it clear that they are seeking a homeland. [15] If they were thinking about where they came from, they would have had an opportunity to return. [16] But they now desire a better place — a heavenly one. Therefore, God is not ashamed to be called their God, for he has prepared a city for them.

THE BEST IS YET TO COME

"The best is yet to come" is a sentiment we often hear at certain momentous occasions in life—high school graduation, a wedding, the beginning of a new career, or the birth of a child. That's because we tend to tie promises of the future to those kinds of important life events. You'd be hard-pressed, though, to find a birthday card for your ninety-year-old grandmother that expresses that same thought.

But that's exactly what we find in Hebrews 11. "These all died" refers to the patriarchs of Israel who were mentioned in the preceding verses and about whom we read last week. The patriarchs lived in faith, and they died in faith, too, even though they hadn't received the things that were promised.

Abraham, for example, only saw one grandson in his earthly life. But that didn't mean God's promise to make him a great nation failed. The promise was in process. That's why Abraham left his home in Ur and lived the majority of his 175 years as a sojourner and foreigner. His eyes weren't fixed on where he had been; they were fixed on a future promise. The result? All nations on earth have now been blessed because Abraham believed that the best was still to come.

In life and in death, faith looks forward.

That's true whether we're nineteen or ninety-nine. We may not see the fulfillment of all of God's promises in our lifetime. Still, faith in Jesus calls us out of comfort to something better and more lasting. Faith is about desiring a better place—a heavenly one. Our faith in what is in front of us will often disappoint. God never will.

Faith looks forward.

REFLECTIONS

Which of God's plans for your future are you looking forward to?

How can we be faithful in the present while also seeking God's faithfulness in the future?

What changes would take place in your life this week if your faith were truly looking forward to God's eternal promises?

HEBREWS 11:17-28

[17] By faith Abraham, when he was tested, offered up Isaac. He received the promises and yet he was offering his one and only son, [18] the one to whom it had been said, **Your offspring will be traced through Isaac.** [19] He considered God to be able even to raise someone from the dead; therefore, he received him back, figuratively speaking.

[20] By faith Isaac blessed Jacob and Esau concerning things to come. [21] By faith Jacob, when he was dying, blessed each of the sons of Joseph, and **he worshiped, leaning on the top of his staff.** [22] By faith Joseph, as he was nearing the end of his life, mentioned the exodus of the Israelites and gave instructions concerning his bones.

[23] By faith Moses, after he was born, was hidden by his parents for three months, because they saw that the child was beautiful, and they didn't fear the king's edict. [24] By faith Moses, when he had grown up, refused to be called the son of Pharaoh's daughter [25] and chose to suffer with the people of God rather than to enjoy the fleeting pleasure of sin. [26] For he considered reproach for the sake of Christ to be greater wealth than the treasures of Egypt, since he was looking ahead to the reward.

[27] By faith he left Egypt behind, not being afraid of the king's anger, for Moses persevered as one who sees him who is invisible. [28] By faith he instituted the Passover and the sprinkling of the blood, so that the destroyer of the firstborn might not touch the Israelites.

THE HOPE OF CERTAIN PROMISE

It's incredibly tempting to shift our focus away from God's promises when we're unsure or uncertain about what is ahead. When we give into that temptation, we turn to inferior objects of faith, like the "promise" of our own abilities, connections, finances, or plans. The people we read about in Hebrews 11 were certainly tempted in those same ways, but they determined to keep their eyes fixed on the promises of God.

All the great stories we read about in the Old Testament are people who were guided by faith in Jesus toward the hope of God's promises.

Abraham didn't know what God was planning to do when he offered up Isaac. He only had an idea about what God could do. Isaac, Jacob, and Joseph didn't know what God was planning to do through their lineage. Moses's parents didn't know what God was planning to do through their son. Moses himself didn't know what God was planning to do through him. The Israelites didn't know what God was planning to do through them. Rahab didn't know what God was planning to do through her. None of these heroes of the faith knew what was coming next.

And we may not have a clue what is just around the corner for us. But we can rest assured that God knows, and His plan is best.

Does this excite you? Terrify you? Motivate you? Overwhelm you? Does it invoke some other reaction? God always makes a way for those who choose to be guided by faith in Jesus toward the hope of His eternal promises.

Jesus is the only one worthy object of our faith. When we believe God for who He is and what He promises in Christ, He shifts the focus from our inability to His sufficiency. And His sufficiency is more than enough.

You may not know what is just around the corner.
But you can trust that God knows.

REFLECTIONS

Which one of these examples of faith do you find most helpful or encouraging? Why?

Considering how difficult life was for these first-century Hebrew Christians, why do you think the author of Hebrews listed men and women from a time and place long ago to encourage them?

How has your faith challenged you to do something hard? Is doing hard things a requirement for faith? Explain.

HEBREWS 11:32-40

[32] And what more can I say? Time is too short for me to tell about Gideon, Barak, Samson, Jephthah, David, Samuel, and the prophets, [33] who by faith conquered kingdoms, administered justice, obtained promises, shut the mouths of lions, [34] quenched the raging of fire, escaped the edge of the sword, gained strength in weakness, became mighty in battle, and put foreign armies to flight. [35] Women received their dead, raised to life again. Other people were tortured, not accepting release, so that they might gain a better resurrection. [36] Others experienced mockings and scourgings, as well as bonds and imprisonment. [37] They were stoned, they were sawed in two, they died by the sword, they wandered about in sheepskins, in goatskins, destitute, afflicted, and mistreated. [38] The world was not worthy of them. They wandered in deserts and on mountains, hiding in caves and holes in the ground.

[39] All these were approved through their faith, but they did not receive what was promised, [40] since God had provided something better for us, so that they would not be made perfect without us.

THE REAL LIFE OF A HERO

When we think of heroes, we typically think of men and women who serve others in profound ways. A fireman who dashes into a burning building to rescue a child is a hero. A quarterback who, against all odds, leads his injury-ridden team from behind to win the Super Bowl is a hero. A person who risks everything to rescue girls who have been trafficked is a hero.

Being a hero in faith, though, may not always look like we picture it.

Many today ascribe to a version of "faith" that always ends in prosperity. In other words, they believe that if someone is a hero of the faith, that person's life will be marked by financial blessing and physical well-being. But this kind of "faith" is clearly not the story of Scripture.

The "heroes" mentioned here in Hebrews 11 do not have a typical hero's journey. They were often marked by hardship and struggle, but just as often they were marked by the miraculous and supernatural working of God. And God approved of their faith.

Faith is not founded on our circumstances; it is founded on God's character.

All the hardship the writer details in these verses are given profound meaning in verse 40: "God had provided something better." These heroes of the faith didn't have earthly prosperity, because God had something better than earthly prosperity in mind. Isaiah 55:8 puts it this way: God's thoughts are not our thoughts, and His ways are not our ways.

The same is true even now, for those of us who live in the present fulfillment of God's promise of salvation in Jesus Christ. God often redirects our paths, not always in ways we expect, but they always lead to something better.

Faith is not founded on your circumstances;
it is founded on God's character.

REFLECTIONS

How do the portraits of faith in these verses lead you to rethink the term *hero*?

When you're enduring hardship and suffering, what better things can you know God has in store?

How does this passage from Hebrews encourage you in light of your own suffering and the questions of faith that suffering brings on?

HEBREWS 12:1-2

THE CALL TO ENDURANCE

12 Therefore, since we also have such a large cloud of witnesses surrounding us, let us lay aside every hindrance and the sin that so easily ensnares us. Let us run with endurance the race that lies before us, ² keeping our eyes on Jesus, the pioneer and perfecter of our faith. For the joy that lay before him, he endured the cross, despising the shame, and sat down at the right hand of the throne of God.

THE PERFECTER OF FAITH

The author of Hebrews compared the Christian life to a race. Those who have placed faith in Jesus are like athletes striving toward the finish line, with a large crowd of people who have also run that race cheering them on.

But there are two different ways of running that race. Someone running in flip-flops or a long flowing robe wouldn't seem very intent on finishing the race well. Those clothing choices would trip her up or encumber her movement. The runner who has, instead, chosen to set aside those clothes in favor of clothes that enable swiftness and perseverance is what we are to picture here.

This is allegory, of course. Flip-flops and a long flowing robe represent those who place their faith in someone or something besides Jesus. Laying those "clothes" aside, on the other hand, represents someone who determines to place his or her faith in Jesus, who is the better choice by far.

Whatever we have placed our faith in, Jesus is better.

Jesus is the fullness of the hope the people we read about in the Old Testament longed for. He is better than anything they could have imagined and is better still than anything we can create. And He has done more to prove His faithfulness.

No matter how long or short our race is or what it entails, we can persevere knowing that Jesus has secured our victory. He is the pioneer and perfecter of our faith. He has blazed a trail before us.

On the cross, Jesus willingly endured all our brokenness and shame, so that we could lay those things aside. He will always be true and faithful to us, and holds the promise of greater joy ahead.

Because of Jesus, there is nothing that can hinder us as we run to Him.

No matter what your race entails, you can persevere knowing that Jesus has secured your victory.

REFLECTIONS

What does it mean that Jesus went to the cross—an instrument of suffering and death—with joy (v.2)? What does that teach us about who He is?

How does shame trip us up as we "run the race" God has set before us? How does faith in Jesus set aside that hindrance?

The heroes of the faith in Hebrews 11 serve as a "large cloud of witnesses surrounding us." Based on their examples, what would these men and women say to you in your current circumstance?

The Work of Christ

Hebrews consistently points us to the life, death, and resurrection of Christ and the benefits of those realities for those who believe in faith. Hebrews 12:2-4 in particular, points to those specific events. The actions Christ took to secure our salvation are often referred to as the "work of Christ." This week's readings bring several features of His work into focus.

HEBREWS 12:2
Jesus is the pioneer and
perfecter of our faith.

JOHN 6:40; ISAIAH 45:22
It was always God's will to
give eternal life to everyone
who looks in faith to Jesus.

HEBREWS 12:2
Jesus endured the cross,
despising its shame.

LUKE 23:33-46; 1 PETER 2:23-24
Jesus hung on a cross between two
criminals being mocked. All the
while, Jesus committed His spirit
to God and ministered to others.

HEBREWS 12:2
Jesus is seated at
the right hand of
the throne of God.

**LUKE 24:51; ACTS 5:31;
REVELATION 3:21**
After Jesus rose from the grave,
He ascended into heaven as the
Exalted One at God's right hand.

HEBREWS 12:4
Jesus shed His own
blood to rescue us
from sin and death.

JOHN 19:30-42
Jesus died on the cross, then His
side was pierced with a sword
and He was buried in a tomb.

HEBREWS 12:3-6

FATHERLY DISCIPLINE

[3] For consider him who endured such hostility from sinners against himself, so that you won't grow weary and give up. [4] In struggling against sin, you have not yet resisted to the point of shedding your blood. [5] And you have forgotten the exhortation that addresses you as sons:

> My son, do not take the Lord's
>> discipline lightly
> or lose heart when you are reproved by him,
> [6] for the Lord disciplines the one he loves
> and punishes every son he receives.

THE LOVE OF DISCIPLINE

If God loves us then why would He let bad things happen?

It's a common question, and often a hindrance to faith. The writer of Hebrews gives us a different perspective in the answer to that question—Jesus demonstrated His faithfulness *through suffering*. His "bad things" were not evidence that God did not love Him; they were evidence of how much God loves us.

Our trials should not push us away from Jesus. They should draw us nearer to Jesus in faith, because He faced more than we could ever imagine to bring us to Himself.

Our difficulties are God's discipline.

That doesn't mean that God is punishing us for doing something wrong. There are things that happen simply because we live in a world subject to the curse of sin. Terrible things happen to people because the world is broken. Those things are not a punishment from God.

And because God loves us like He does, He doesn't let those things go to waste. He uses them for something better—to develop intimacy with Him and faith in Him. He uses them to produce outcomes for our good.

God's discipline isn't punitive, it's restorative. It's not oppressive, it's transformative. He's not mad at us. Trials in our lives are a sign of God's determined love.

He is our Father, and we are His children. He isn't like an earthly parent. He knows what He's doing all the time. He never goes overboard in disciplining us, and He never undershoots either. Neither does He ever neglect our discipline, because He is perfect and all-knowing and He loves us.

Trials in your life are a sign of God's determined love.

REFLECTIONS

Why should we think of discipline from God as corrective rather than a punishment? When have you learned something through discipline?

How do we learn to recognize God's discipline and embrace when He is trying to guide, teach, and correct us?

What would it look like for you to be more receptive to the intention of God's discipline in seasons of hardship and struggle?

PAUSE & LISTEN

Spend some time reflecting over the week's reading.

Let us run with endurance
the race that lies before us,
keeping our eyes on Jesus, the
pioneer and perfecter of our faith.

HEBREWS 12:1-2

REFLECTION

Use these questions for personal reflection or group discussion on Hebrews 11:13–12:6.

What stuck out to you most in this week's reading? What surprised you? Confused you?

What does this week's Scripture teach you about God and His character?

What does this week's Scripture teach you about humanity and our need for grace?

How does this week's Scripture point you to Jesus?

What steps of faith and obedience is God asking you to take through these Scriptures?

PRAY

Pause for a moment and call to mind a few things God has done for you. Spend a few more moments thanking God for His work in your life.

WEEK 6

BETTER ENDURANCE

Don't turn away. Endure.

The sermon recorded in the book of Hebrews concludes the way many sermons do—by recalling the main point and then giving clarity for how we are to apply that truth to daily life.

The preacher had used Scripture to remind his audience that Jesus is a better source, leader, hope, and access to the Father than anyone or anything else they could this day choose or one future day discover. He offered numerous examples of faith to spur them on in theirs. Then in chapters 12 and 13 he brings those realities to the current situation.

Because Jesus is better, don't turn away from Him but endure in faith and obedience.

To live that way in any and every circumstance, we must shift our gaze away from the worldly perspective of suffering and toward God's loving discipline in it.

We must remember that He is holy and His purpose in our lives is equally holy.

We must lift our eyes from earth to heaven and orient our daily steps according to the promise of that eternal home.

No matter what choices lie before us in the difficult experiences of life we'll face, the way of Jesus is better . . . and He will help us endure.

HEBREWS 12:7-13

[7] Endure suffering as discipline: God is dealing with you as sons. For what son is there that a father does not discipline? [8] But if you are without discipline — which all receive — then you are illegitimate children and not sons. [9] Furthermore, we had human fathers discipline us, and we respected them. Shouldn't we submit even more to the Father of spirits and live? [10] For they disciplined us for a short time based on what seemed good to them, but he does it for our benefit, so that we can share his holiness. [11] No discipline seems enjoyable at the time, but painful. Later on, however, it yields the peaceful fruit of righteousness to those who have been trained by it.

[12] Therefore, strengthen your tired hands and weakened knees, [13] and make straight paths for your feet, so that what is lame may not be dislocated but healed instead.

ANY MEANS NECESSARY

God is our Father and He loves us. As such, He wants to help us grow and mature. He isn't only interested in our future life with Him in heaven. He wants to help us experience spiritual health in the present.

Think of it this way—parents don't put vegetables on their children's plates to punish them. They put vegetables on their children's plates because if they never eat vegetables their health and well-being will be at risk. The vegetables, though often unenjoyable, serve a good purpose. As the children grow older, they may even begin to like vegetables.

God guides His children as a father guides a son, through discipline—allowing us to face unwanted circumstances and experiences. We might resist, but He does it out of love. God's discipline gives way to spiritual health and well-being.

You might be wondering why this distinction matters. After all, a struggle is a struggle; it's hard, and you just want it to end.

Understanding that your difficulty is God's discipline is an important shift in perspective. If you think about it as a passing moment, you run the risk of never allowing God to change you. If you think of your struggle just as something you have to get through for life to get better again, without acknowledging that God has purpose in it, then it's likely you're going to miss out on that purpose—the "fruit of righteousness" (v. 11) He intends to produce in you.

Endurance isn't simply getting to the other side of the struggle. Endurance is learning and growing in the struggle, in faith—joining God in His good purpose of increasing your spiritual health, by any means necessary.

Endurance is about far more than simply getting to the other side of your struggle.

REFLECTIONS

Remember that these Hebrews were considering giving up and turning back to Judaism. In Hebrews 12:7-13, what did the writer want them to understand?

How does knowing that God is our perfect Father help us understand the kind of discipline described in this passage?

Think about the discipline—the circumstances and experiences in your life—that God is calling you to endure. Based on this passage, what will be the end result?

HEBREWS 12:14-17

WARNING AGAINST REJECTING GOD'S GRACE

[14] Pursue peace with everyone, and holiness — without it no one will see the Lord. [15] Make sure that no one falls short of the grace of God and that no root of bitterness springs up, causing trouble and defiling many. [16] And make sure that there isn't any immoral or irreverent person like Esau, who sold his birthright in exchange for a single meal. [17] For you know that later, when he wanted to inherit the blessing, he was rejected, even though he sought it with tears, because he didn't find any opportunity for repentance.

ALIGNING OUR LIVES

If a person continues to fail at achieving an outcome of success, it is often said to be due to a lack of discipline—behaving in a controlled way to obey a set of rules or standards.

The writer of Hebrews, though, wanted his readers to understand that God's spiritual discipline would never leave them lacking.

Because of Jesus, none of us lacks discipline. What we are in danger of lacking, though, is the humility needed to develop endurance in that discipline. As the first ten chapters of Hebrews reminded us, Jesus is better than everything else, including our own efforts.

We do not find success with God through self-discipline to follow a set of rules. Instead, God's discipline in our lives guides us into spiritual habits that align our lives with His character.

We do have personal responsibility in receiving and applying that discipline, though. To illustrate this, the author of Hebrews pulls in another Old Testament example (see Genesis 25:27-34). Esau's foolish behavior certainly wasn't because God didn't love him or discipline him as a son. In fact, Esau's hunger was evidence of God's discipline in his life. And Esau chose poorly, dismissing the greater blessing in favor of instantly gratifying his hunger.

We all face this same danger. To help us avoid it, there is a measure of accountability in community described in these verses. For better endurance, God gives us each other.

Our response to God's discipline impacts our transformation toward peace and holiness and also the transformation of other people.

God's discipline in your life guides you into habits of holiness that impact the community of faith.

REFLECTIONS

What habits of holiness is God working to guide you toward? How? (Ex. God allows you to give yourself over to busyness to the point of exhaustion so that you will learn to prioritize the practice of resting in Him.)

Reread verses 15-16. How is the community of faith meant to help you endure?

How are you meant to help others in the community of faith endure? What attitude does those instructions require of you?

INSIGHTS

Hebrews isn't the only New Testament book to encourage believers to face the Lord's discipline with endurance. For example, James wrote, "Consider it great joy . . . when you experience various trials, because you know that the testing of your faith produces endurance. And let endurance have its full effect, so that you may be mature and complete, lacking nothing" (James 1:2-4). And Peter wrote that we should not be surprised when suffering comes but should know that Christ will "restore, establish, strengthen, and support you after you have suffered a little while" (1 Peter 4:12; 5:10).

HEBREWS 12:18-29

[18] For you have not come to what could be touched, to a blazing fire, to darkness, gloom, and storm, [19] to the blast of a trumpet, and the sound of words. Those who heard it begged that not another word be spoken to them, [20] for they could not bear what was commanded: **If even an animal touches the mountain, it must be stoned.** [21] The appearance was so terrifying that Moses said, **I am trembling with fear.** [22] Instead, you have come to Mount Zion, to the city of the living God (the heavenly Jerusalem), to myriads of angels, a festive gathering, [23] to the assembly of the firstborn whose names have been written in heaven, to a Judge, who is God of all, to the spirits of righteous people made perfect, [24] and to Jesus, the mediator of a new covenant, and to the sprinkled blood, which says better things than the blood of Abel.

[25] See to it that you do not reject the one who speaks. For if they did not escape when they rejected him who warned them on earth, even less will we if we turn away from him who warns us from heaven. [26] His voice shook the earth at that time, but now he has promised, **Yet once more I will shake not only the earth but also the heavens.** [27] This expression, "Yet once more," indicates the removal of what can be shaken — that is, created things — so that what is not shaken might remain. [28] Therefore, since we are receiving a kingdom that cannot be shaken, let us be thankful. By it, we may serve God acceptably, with reverence and awe, [29] for our God is a consuming fire.

DAY 38

IN UNSHAKABLE HOLINESS

As we serve God, we need to remain mindful of the one we are serving. He is good and gracious, and also holy. Holy is a word used to describe God's absolute moral perfection and otherness. No one and nothing is like God.

Verse 26 reminds us of the depth of God's holiness—His voice caused an earthquake (Exodus 19:18). As God's holiness was tangibly manifested in their presence, the people were terrified.

When it comes to earthquakes and other disasters, many people tend to think Satan is at work. And certainly he wants to use those disasters for his purposes, but God in His sovereignty is doing a better, more enduring work. He allows such things to take place to warn us, and to remind us to trust and serve Him only.

It's the same when He allows our personal circumstances to shake. God's holiness and grace are in the shaking, so that we'll hold onto Him, the Unshakable One. We take our devotion seriously because God is worthy of our devotion.

Every single struggle is an opportunity for God to bring us to a place of deeper wonder about who He is—not deeper worry, but deeper wonder.

We don't stand terrified before God at Mt. Sinai like the Israelites did. Because of our relationship to Jesus, we stand before God in confident endurance. We stand before Him in view of Mount Zion, our heavenly eternal home, where we will dwell forever in His perfect holiness and grace.

He will shake every single one of our earthly affections. But He is unshakable. His kingdom, promised to His children, is unshakable. His grace is unshakable. His purpose for us is unshakable. So we can be thankful, and serve Him willingly, with reverence and awe.

God is worthy of your devotion.

REFLECTIONS

List the words in these verses that are used to describe God and God's power.

Read Psalm 46:2-3,6. How does Hebrews 12:26-29 explain why the psalmist said, "Therefore we will not be afraid"?

What is something in your life that God likely wants to shake? For what purpose might He do that?

HEBREWS 13:1-6

FINAL EXHORTATIONS

13 Let brotherly love continue. [2] Don't neglect to show hospitality, for by doing this some have welcomed angels as guests without knowing it. [3] Remember those in prison, as though you were in prison with them, and the mistreated, as though you yourselves were suffering bodily. [4] Marriage is to be honored by all and the marriage bed kept undefiled, because God will judge the sexually immoral and adulterers. [5] Keep your life free from the love of money. Be satisfied with what you have, for he himself has said, **I will never leave you or abandon you.** [6] Therefore, we may boldly say,

> **The Lord is my helper;**
>
> **I will not be afraid.**
>
> **What can man do to me?**

HELPING OUR NEED

In this last chapter of Hebrews, the author offers final exhortations. These are brief but provide direction and takeaways from what we've spent time reading.

Hebrews 13:1-6 touches on various subjects about which we might struggle to endure in obedience to Christ—brotherly love, hospitality, empathy for those who are imprisoned or mistreated, marriage, issues of sexual immorality, and money.

We can sum it up this way: because Jesus is better, we should endure in faith, and because faith necessitates action, we should endure in obedience, too. As the Hebrew Christians were discovering, that's not easy. But a reality far greater than the difficulty was theirs to experience—the Lord was their helper (v. 6).

In all the ways they were struggling to apply relationship with Jesus in daily life, the Lord would help them. They didn't need to be afraid. To recognize Jesus as the better starting point for knowing God's provision when distracted by issues of wealth, the Lord would help. To follow Jesus as the better leader in marriage and other relationships, He would help. To rest in Jesus as the better hope when mistreated or imprisoned, He would help. To depend on Jesus as the better access to God when conflict got in the way of brotherly love, He would help. To find in Jesus better faith and endurance when tempted to give up, He would help.

We come to Jesus believing He is better. But then, somewhere along the way, we are tempted toward self-sufficiency. We think we have to work it out ourselves.

But it's good to be needy.

The beauty of our relationship with the Lord is our need for the Lord. He gives us His help, and His help gives us confidence to endure. But to receive that help, we must boldly turn to Him.

It's good to be needy.

REFLECTIONS

The author starts his conclusion by summarizing the letter's main points. How would you summarize the content of Hebrews, having read through most of it?

Is it easy for you to ask God for help? Why or why not?

What is appealing about being self-sufficient? As followers of Jesus, why is it important to constantly recognize our need for Him?

Discipline
& Endurance

The themes of discipline and endurance found in Hebrews are connected strongly throughout the Bible. Recognizing themes in different places within Scripture will train us to be better readers of the Bible and deepen our knowledge of and devotion to God.

HEBREWS 12:11
Godly discipline produces
righteousness for those who
are trained by it.

2 CORINTHIANS 12:7-10
Paul was given a "thorn" that he prayed God
would remove. Instead, God showed Paul
His grace and power through that difficulty.

HEBREWS 12:29
God is worthy of reverence
and awe. He is a
consuming fire.

EXODUS 19:18
God descended on Mount Sinai in fire
with a trumpet blast and an earthquake.
JOEL 3:16
God's voice causes the heavens
and earth to shake.

HEBREWS 13:2
Godly endurance manifests
itself in hospitality,
even to strangers.

GENESIS 17:27-18:10
In the heat of the day after being circumcised,
Abraham hurried to show hospitality to three
strangers, who turned out to be angels.

HEBREWS 13:14
This world is temporary;
we must fix our eyes on
our eternal home.

JEREMIAH 29:14
God promised to gather His people
and bring them back from captivity.
1 PETER 2:11-12
God uses the enduring faithfulness of His
exiles here on earth for His eternal glory.

HEBREWS 13:7-21

[7] Remember your leaders who have spoken God's word to you. As you carefully observe the outcome of their lives, imitate their faith. [8] Jesus Christ is the same yesterday, today, and forever. [9] Don't be led astray by various kinds of strange teachings; for it is good for the heart to be established by grace and not by food regulations, since those who observe them have not benefited. [10] We have an altar from which those who worship at the tabernacle do not have a right to eat. [11] For the bodies of those animals whose blood is brought into the most holy place by the high priest as a sin offering are burned outside the camp. [12] Therefore, Jesus also suffered outside the gate, so that he might sanctify the people by his own blood. [13] Let us, then, go to him outside the camp, bearing his disgrace. [14] For we do not have an enduring city here; instead, we seek the one to come. [15] Therefore, through him let us continually offer up to God a sacrifice of praise, that is, the fruit of lips that confess his name. [16] Don't neglect to do what is good and to share, for God is pleased with such sacrifices. [17] Obey your leaders and submit to them, since they keep watch over your souls as those who will give an account, so that they can do this with joy and not with grief, for that would be unprofitable for you. [18] Pray for us, for we are convinced that we have a clear conscience, wanting to conduct ourselves honorably in everything. [19] And I urge you all the more to pray that I may be restored to you very soon.

BENEDICTION AND FAREWELL

[20] Now may the God of peace, who brought up from the dead our Lord Jesus — the great Shepherd of the sheep — through the blood of the everlasting covenant, [21] equip you with everything good to do his will, working in us what is pleasing in his sight, through Jesus Christ, to whom be glory forever and ever. Amen.

REORIENTING OUR VIEW

The book of Hebrews ends with the practical application of the truth in which it begins—Jesus Christ is better than everyone and everything.

The fact of Jesus's outright superiority will never change.

Jesus was the same when these Hebrews were considering turning back to Judaism as He was when they had turned to Him in faith from Judaism. No matter what life held for them, Jesus would remain forever the same as He has always been.

There would be difficult times. These followers of Jesus were not home yet. The exile of their ancestors in places like Egypt and Babylon was meant to serve as a picture of their own "exile"—the time in between. Until the day they would stand before Jesus in heaven, they would live and die in exile.

This is true of every follower of Jesus in every time and culture.

So we need to listen to those who speak God's Word to us and beware of fads and flashy teachers whose promises of a better way are a dangerous trap.

We do not have an enduring city here, but we seek the one to come. Hebrews reminds us to lift our eyes up to heaven and use the view of heaven to reorient our lives right now.

With heaven in view, we offer God our praise, do what is good, share with others, obey and submit to leaders, and, with our hope fixed on Jesus, continually pray for the advancement of God's kingdom on earth.

What Jesus has promised and what He is bringing is better.

Use the view of heaven to
reorient your life in the here and now.

REFLECTIONS

What was the most meaningful thing you learned studying Hebrews?

How should the truth that Jesus is the same yesterday, today, and forever affect the way you trust Him in the day-to-day?

There will be times when you, like the Hebrew Christians, are tempted to fix your eyes on temporary, earthly circumstances instead of your enduring, eternal, better home in heaven. What are some practical steps you can take to reorient your view?

PAUSE & LISTEN
Spend some time reflecting over the week's reading.

For we do not have an
enduring city here; instead,
we seek the one to come.

HEBREWS 13:14

REFLECTION

Use these questions for personal reflection or group discussion on Hebrews 12:7–13:21.

What stuck out to you most in this week's reading? What surprised you? Confused you?

What does this week's Scripture teach you about God and His character?

What does this week's Scripture teach you about humanity and our need for grace?

How does this week's Scripture point you to Jesus?

What steps of faith and obedience is God asking you to take through these Scriptures?

PRAY

End your time in Hebrews worshiping God. Praise God for accomplishing our redemption and bringing us out of slavery to sin and death.

PHOTOGRAPHY CREDITS

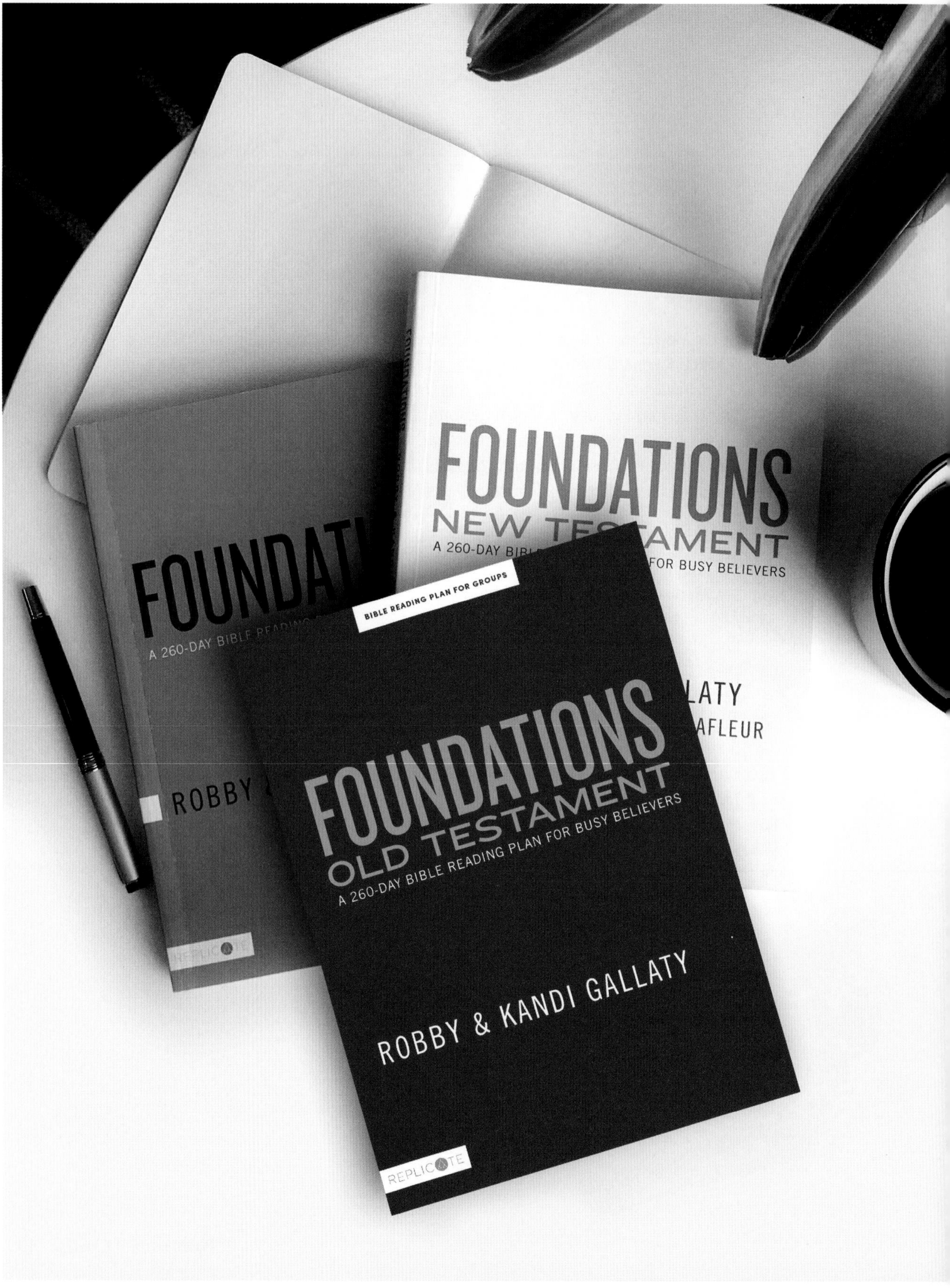
FOUNDATIONS
BIBLE READING PLAN FOR GROUPS
FOUNDATIONS
OLD TESTAMENT
A 260-DAY BIBLE READING PLAN FOR BUSY BELIEVERS
ROBBY & KANDI GALLATY
REPLICATE

Manageable one-year plans for Bible reading

Foundations gives you a one-year Bible reading plan that requires just five days of study per week to fit your busy schedule. It includes daily devotional material. And through the HEAR journaling method, you'll learn how to Highlight, Explain, Apply, and Respond to passages, allowing for practical application.

Foundations
Study key passages of the Bible in one year,
while still having the flexibility of reading five days per week.

005769893 **$14.99**

Foundations: New Testament
Read and reflect on the New Testament in one year
with this reading and devotional guide.

005810327 **$14.99**

Foundations: Old Testament
Read through the story of the Old Testament in one year
using this manageable five-day-per-week plan.

005831469 **$14.99**

lifeway.com/foundations
Learn more online or call 800.458.2772.

EXPERIENCING
GOD

SOME STUDIES HELP YOU KNOW THE BIBLE.
THIS ONE HELPS YOU KNOW THE AUTHOR.

For more than three decades, God has used the truths of *Experiencing God* to awaken believers to a radically God-centered way of life. As a result, millions have come to know God intimately, to recognize His voice, and to understand His will for their lives. This new edition is revised, updated, and ready to lead you again—or for the very first time—into a deeper relationship with God.

THE JOURNEY TO
CHRIST BEGINS HERE

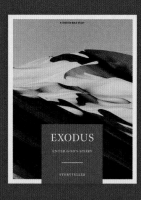

Exodus is the rosetta stone for unlocking the Old Testament and the thread of redemption throughout Scripture. In this inaugural volume of the Storyteller series, you will walk through the first 15 chapters of Exodus. Relive the experience as God hears the cries of His people and responds by sending a deliverer, ultimately giving us a pattern for recognizing His work in the world.

Learn more online or call 800.458.2772.
lifeway.com/storyteller

Is anything better than Jesus?

There are many similarities to the Christians of today and those who lived in biblical times. We don't fit neatly into the culture. And the more we live for Jesus, the harder life can get. It's easy to want to compromise. But should we?

The writer of Hebrews recognized this same tendency in the people of his day. Following Jesus's leadership meant great personal sacrifice. So they considered other leaders and wondered if following Jesus was the best option.

We are all prone to get sidetracked by other ideas we find interesting. Our eyes drift away from Jesus and fix themselves on other leaders. And so Hebrews calls us to consider Jesus again and again. Because every time we do, we'll see that there is no better option.

This six-session Bible study is designed to help you:

- Understand key themes from Hebrews.
- See yourself in the story of Jesus.
- Learn that Jesus is better than anything else in your life.
- See how Hebrews presents key themes from the Old Testament in a New Testament light.

ADDITIONAL RESOURCES

eBOOK
Includes the content of this printed book but offers the convenience and flexibility that come with mobile technology.

005837546 **$19.99**

Storyteller resources can be found online at lifeway.com/storyteller

Price and availability subject to change without notice.